Red, White, and Disney

The Myths and Realities of American History at the Walt Disney World Resort

Brittany DiCologero

Theme Park Press
The Happiest Books on Earth
www.ThemeParkPress.com

© **2018 Brittany DiCologero**

No part of this publication may be reproduced, distributed, or transmitted in any form or by any means, including photocopying, recording, or other electronic or mechanical methods, without the prior written permission of the publisher, except for brief quotations embodied in critical reviews and certain other non-commercial uses permitted by copyright law.

Although every precaution has been taken to verify the accuracy of the information contained herein, no responsibility is assumed for any errors or omissions, and no liability is assumed for damages that may result from the use of this information.

Theme Park Press is not associated with the Walt Disney Company.

The views expressed in this book are those of the author and do not necessarily reflect the views of Theme Park Press.

Theme Park Press publishes its books in a variety of print and electronic formats. Some content that appears in one format may not appear in another.

Editor: Bob McLain
Layout: Artisanal Text

ISBN 978-1-68390-131-0
Printed in the United States of America

Theme Park Press | www.ThemeParkPress.com
Address queries to bob@themeparkpress.com

Contents

ONE
Main Street, U.S.A. 1

TWO
Liberty Square 25

THREE
Frontierland 49

FOUR
Adventureland 67

FIVE
Tomorrowland 71

SIX
Fantasyland 79

SEVEN
Epcot 87

EIGHT
The American Adventure 93

NINE
Disney's Hollywood Studios 119

TEN
Hollywood Boulevard 121

ELEVEN
Sunset Boulevard 127

TWELVE
Echo Lake 133

THIRTEEN
DinoLand U.S.A. 137

FOURTEEN
Magic Kingdom Area Resorts 145

FIFTEEN
Epcot Area Resorts 161

SIXTEEN
Disney Springs Area Resorts 165

SEVENTEEN
Everything Else 169

Epilogue 171

Acknowledgments 173

About the Author 175

About Theme Park Press 177

CHAPTER ONE
Main Street, U.S.A.

Main Street, U.S.A. The re-created vision in the Magic Kingdom of Walt Disney's childhood home of Marceline, Missouri. Although we are told that Marceline was where Walt grew up, his family only had a farm in the town for five years early in Walt's life. Walt was born in Chicago on December 5, 1901, to Elias and Flora Disney who moved to Marceline five years later, in 1906. The Disneys operated a farm in Marceline until 1910, when Elias struggled with a number of health issues that forced them to sell the farm and move to Kansas City.

With Walt leaving Marceline before he turned ten years old, the town must have left a lasting impression for him to base one of the most important parts of Disneyland (and subsequent parks) around it. Long after his stay in Marceline, Walt was quoted in a *Marceline News* article stating:

> To tell the truth, more things of importance happened to me in Marceline than have happened since—or are likely to in the future.

What was it about Marceline that left such an impression? Of course Marceline drives home the traditional "small town America" sort of feeling, with its small family-owned businesses lining picturesque streets, but was this enough to serve as the basis for the first land guests would see when entering Disneyland? To Walt it was.

1893 Chicago World's Fair

Main Street, U.S.A. transports guests back to the turn of the century. Set approximately between 1890 and 1910, the street reminds us of a time when traditional ways of life were still held to a high standard, but technological advances in numerous fields were steadily becoming more valuable factors in the lives of everyday Americans. Referred to by Disney Imagineer Eddie Sotto as "a living history museum of real America," many of the props guests see today while exploring Main Street are authentic antiques from the time period. Walt Disney described the time period represented by Disneyland's Main Street:

> Soon the gas light will be replaced by electricity, but that was still in the future. ... At this time, little Main Street was still the most important spot in the nation, combining the color of frontier days with the oncoming excitement of the new 20th century.

And in fact Main Street features both gas lights and electric lamps, to signal the change in technology taking place in that exact moment in time.

While each area of Walt Disney World is intricately themed, there are few locations where we are able to pin down a concrete period that the Imagineers had in mind when designing the park. A walk through some of the businesses on Main Street can give us a glimpse into some solid evidence that the World's Columbian Exposition—or the 1893 Chicago World's Fair, as it was also known—has just recently taken place.

Our best guess for when exactly Main Street, U.S.A. is in relation to the fair would be closer to 1900. Though the area is influenced by the fair, it is worth noting that information took much longer to travel during the late 19th century. Within one or two years after the fair, most American citizens were probably not fully aware of what the fair accomplished. Consider the fact that Alexander Graham Bell's famous phone call only took place 17 years prior to the fair in 1876, and you can imagine how information was still being conveyed to the public during this time. Telephones were available for consumer use within the next couple of years, but early switchboards could only hold two or three conversations at a time. Although the telephone was a pre-Chicago World's Fair sign of progress, communications regarding the details of the World's Fair would not reach the general public immediately.

The 1893 Chicago World's Fair was one of the first times that popular household products we still use today were exhibited. These were goods that would have had a lasting impact not only on the residents of Walt's real and fictional Main Street,

U.S.A., but also things that we know from our own daily lives to be extremely useful. Of these items, the most popular household appliances that had early previews at the fair were dishwashers and fluorescent lightbulbs. It is not outlandish to think that some of the businesses on Main Street would soon enjoy having dishwashers and fluorescent lights.

Some of the other "firsts" exhibited at the fair are ironically not to be found anywhere near Main Street. Wrigley's chewing gum first made its public appearance at the fair, as did Pabst Blue Ribbon beer—two goods which are not sold on Main Street. The Wrigley's gum first produced for the fair can still be purchased today as Juicy Fruit, America's first mass-produced chewing gum. Prior to the fair, Pabst Blue Ribbon beer was called Best Select. It was brewed out of Milwaukee by German immigrant Jacob Best, who updated the name after his product won the blue ribbon at the 1893 Chicago World's Fair. Today, Walt Disney World does not sell chewing gum in any of its shops, and alcohol has only been (legally) consumed inside the Magic Kingdom since 2012, at select restaurants.

Nods to the Chicago World's Fair may be found all over Main Street. Though the atmosphere is classic, small town America, there are some hints that the Industrial Revolution is right around the corner. The average guest probably spends more time looking at the products for sale than at the stores themselves while perusing the shops on Main Street, but if you take the time to look above some of the shelves you'll see some items that were being exhibited during the Fair. Shops like Crystal Arts and the Main Street Confectionery are decorated with both props and images from the Fair. From the candy-sorting devices that may be seen on the ceiling of the confectionery to the smaller images and pieces of artwork laced throughout the rest of Main Street, there are a variety of ways that we can see the fair as inspiration for Main Street's design just from walking through the area.

The confectionery comes with another lesser-known backstory in relation to the fair. You may notice the name "Thomas McCrumb" listed as the proprietor of the store. In Walt's younger days, McCrumb was his dentist. The storyline of the shop follows McCrumb as he attended the 1893 World's

Fair, and became fascinated with the machinery he saw there. Inspired, he brought the same technology home to automate production in his candy shop, which guests can see today hanging above the merchandise.

One invention that debuted during the 1893 Chicago World's Fair can be found not only on Main Street but at numerous locations throughout Walt Disney World: the penny press. The first known penny press machine debuted at the fair and featured a simple design of text reading "Chicago World's Fair 1893." Today, penny presses are prevalent not only in Disney theme parks, but in aquariums, zoos, museums, national parks, and other businesses and tourist attractions across the globe.

Another interesting note about the 1893 Chicago World's Fair is that Elias Disney, Walt's father, worked as a carpenter at the fair. It is unclear if this fact served as further motivation for Main Street to be designed around this time period, but it does continue the slew of connections that the fair has to Main Street and Walt Disney's childhood in Marceline, Missouri.

There is one more byproduct of the fair that is connected to Main Street, but perhaps only by pure coincidence. According to legend propagated by the creators of Cracker Jack, Loius and Frederick William Rueckheim, Cracker Jacks were sold at the 1893 Chicago World's Fair. Their claim may be apocryphal, as no known evidence exists for the popular snack having been sold there. While the two brothers claim that their product was available at the fair, all other evidence seems to confirm that Cracker Jack was instead created in 1896, the same year the name of the snack was patented. What is the connection to Main Street, U.S.A. if Cracker Jack is not a consequence of the fair? We'll need to take a walk down to Casey's Corner to find out.

"Casey at the Bat"

Casey's Corner, the baseball-themed quick-service restaurant at the end of Main Street, is not only home to Cracker Jack, but to all things baseball—all things turn-of-the-century baseball that can fit into a small quick service restaurant, that is.

Casey's Corner is inspired by the classic poem "Casey at the Bat" by 19th century American poet Ernest Thayer. The title character, Casey, is believed to be the determining factor in whether or not the poem's home team from the town of "Mudville" will win the game. Thayer has claimed that "the poem has no basis in fact"; however, a couple of towns have since recalled their neighborhoods of Mudville as the location that inspired the poem. Stockton, California, was known as Mudville until 1850 when it was incorporated, and Holliston, Massachusetts, to this day has a neighborhood called Mudville. Both towns would seem like probable guesses (if not disputed by the author himself) as Thayer covered Stockton's local baseball during his stint as a journalist, and he is from Worcester, Massachusetts.

More important for one of our favorite quick-service restaurants, however, is the poem itself, "Casey at the Bat: A Ballad of the Republic Sung in the Year 1888":

> The outlook wasn't brilliant for the Mudville nine that day:
> The score stood four to two, with but one inning more to play,
> And then when Cooney died at first, and Barrows did the same
> A pall-like silence fell upon the patrons of the game.
>
> A straggling few got up to go in deep despair. The rest
> Clung to the hope which springs eternal in the human breast;
> They thought, "If only Casey could but get a whack at that—
> We'd put up even money now, with Casey at the bat."
>
> But Flynn preceded Casey, as did also Jimmy Blake,
> And the former was a hoodoo, while the latter was a cake;
> So upon that stricken multitude grim melancholy sat,
> For there seemed but little chance of Casey getting to the bat.
>
> But Flynn let drive a single, to the wonderment of all,
> And Blake, the much despisèd, tore the cover off the ball;
> And when the dust had lifted, and men saw what had occurred,
> There was Jimmy safe at second and Flynn a-hugging third.
>
> Then from five thousand throats and more there rose a lusty yell;
> It rumbled through the valley, it rattled in the dell;
> It pounded on the mountain and recoiled upon the flat,
> For Casey, mighty Casey, was advancing to the bat.
>
> There was ease in Casey's manner as he stepped into his place;
> There was pride in Casey's bearing and a smile lit Casey's face.
> And when, responding to the cheers, he lightly doffed his hat,
> No stranger in the crowd could doubt 'twas Casey at the bat.

Ten thousand eyes were on him as he rubbed his hands with dirt;
Five thousand tongues applauded when he wiped them on his shirt;
Then while the writhing pitcher ground the ball into his hip,
Defiance flashed in Casey's eye, a sneer curled Casey's lip.

And now the leather-covered sphere came hurtling through the air,
And Casey stood a-watching it in haughty grandeur there.
Close by the sturdy batsman the ball unheeded sped—
"That ain't my style," said Casey. "Strike one!" the umpire said.

From the benches, black with people, there went up a muffled roar,
Like the beating of the storm-waves on a stern and distant shore;
"Kill him! Kill the umpire!" shouted someone on the stand;
And it's likely they'd have killed him had not Casey raised his hand.

With a smile of Christian charity great Casey's visage shone;
He stilled the rising tumult; he bade the game go on;
He signaled to the pitcher, and once more the dun sphere flew;
But Casey still ignored it and the umpire said, "Strike two!"

"Fraud!" cried the maddened thousands, and echo answered "Fraud!"
But one scornful look from Casey and the audience was awed.
They saw his face grow stern and cold, they saw his muscles strain,
And they knew that Casey wouldn't let that ball go by again.

The sneer is gone from Casey's lip, his teeth are clenched in hate,
He pounds with cruel violence his bat upon the plate;
And now the pitcher holds the ball, and now he lets it go,
And now the air is shattered by the force of Casey's blow.

Oh, somewhere in this favoured land the sun is shining bright,
The band is playing somewhere, and somewhere hearts are light;
And somewhere men are laughing, and somewhere children shout,
But there is no joy in Mudville—mighty Casey has struck out.

The fans of the home team looked to Casey as the player who was going to lead Mudville to victory. In the moments before Casey is at the bat, Thayer writes about the fans' actions and emotions in a way that most families who have ever watched a baseball game together can relate to.

The focus of course is the game, but there is much more to the complete experience of enjoying baseball. Part of the experience (in baseball or in watching any sport) is rallying with other fans. It is the spirit of reacting together in celebratory wins, or consoling each other during difficult losses, that makes the baseball community so special. The sports community is not an aspect of the game that is often represented in literature at all, never mind in relatively short poetry, making Thayer's work rather unique in that respect.

While Casey's Corner is "baseball themed," in terms of what the Magic Kingdom stands for the restaurant is also family themed, in a more nostalgic way than many other Disney restaurants would be able to claim. Casey's offers a sense of nostalgia to many families who have been visiting Walt Disney World for years. When I think of Casey's Corner, I remember being a kid on Main Street waiting for the afternoon parade to start, while one of the grown-ups rushed over to grab hot dogs so we could have lunch while we waited. For a family visiting the parks for the first time, Casey's may remind them of the times they've spent together watching "America's pastime."

More than the obvious baseball theme fitting into the time period of Main Street, and anything described as "small-town America," baseball is part of America's collective memory. Even guests visiting the park who have no interest in baseball will be familiar enough with the sport to make sense of the restaurant's theme and location on Main Street. And while they may not relate to Thayer's musings about the baseball community, they will certainly walk out of the Magic Kingdom at the end of the night having felt similar emotions with their friends and family.

Victorian Ideals

Other hints of turn-of-the-century America on Main Street may be found in the intricate attention to detail in the architecture of the buildings. As with many areas in Disney theme parks, Main Street is designed using a forced perspective, meaning that the design of the buildings decrease in height as the eye moves up. The buildings on Main Street, U.S.A. are close together and symmetrical, especially when compared to other areas of the park, a design style typical of the late Victorian era. The close proximity and symmetry of the buildings on Main Street is even more apparent when considering the different themes and building styles in Frontierland and Liberty Square.

Creams, pastels, and brick-red colors were all popular during this period as well. Although we may think of buildings from the turn of the century as having a more diluted paint scheme, our preconceptions are actually due to how these buildings have been maintained and renovated. During the budding years of towns like Marceline, Missouri, or any Main Street, U.S.A., buildings would have been regularly spruced up with the latest and brightest of their traditional color palettes.

An additional detail that the majority of guests likely do not dwell on while visiting Main Street is the inclusion of gender roles in the area's décor. These implications are most evident in the window displays by the Emporium, though they may also be seen throughout all of the businesses on Main Street. The windows closer to the women's sections of the stores are often more heavily decorated with floral and lace details, whereas the other side of the Emporium which includes the men's section is designed with darker wooden elements and a vintage athletic personality in mind—making it reasonable to believe that the men's clothing in the shop is located next to the interior entrance of Casey's Corner.

Main Street, like a number of other locations around Walt Disney World, serves to represent an idealized version of America. While describing Disney's Hollywood Studios (then Disney-MGM Studios) during the park's dedication ceremonies in 1989, then chairman and CEO of the Walt Disney Company Michael Eisner referred to the new park as "not a place on a map, but a state of mind that exists wherever people dream and wonder and imagine." Though Eisner was specifically referring to Disney's Hollywood Studios, this method of thinking can refer to other locations at Disney World, including Main Street, particularly in understanding these areas as representations of American history.

Eisner's description of old Hollywood as a place that "never was but always will be" works just the same for Main Street. Regardless of one's location within the United States, it is not impossible to imagine another town that is at least somewhat similar to Main Street in terms of embracing the small-town classic Americana feel that the park provides guests. The difference comes with realities that for obvious reasons would not be represented in a theme park. Not all but many small towns would not have the opulent style that some buildings on Main Street exhibit. Many real-life Main Streets would also include the necessary eyesores that come with running a town, including dirt roads, horse droppings, garbage, and in some cases, miles of powerlines, all of which have no place in an idealized theme park setting.

Furthermore, consider that by 2016 the average income per capita in the United States was just under $57,000, and the reported income per capita in Marceline was only about $16,500. Marceline has a lower cost of living and other factors that differentiate it from other towns across America, but the dip in per-capita income does illustrate the fact that real-life Marceline is not as well-off as the Magic Kingdom portrays it as being. In fact, Marceline has outlived other similar towns in the area, and Disney's connection is without a doubt one of the driving factors keeping the town afloat today. "We [Marceline] have a lot of community pride. We still have that magic that Walt sensed the moment he stepped off the train in 1905," says then tour director of Marceline Kaye Malins during a *New York Times Interview* in 1998. With the relocation of the town's railroad station in 1986, costing about 100 Marceline residents their job, and the later economic recession in the 2000s not making life any easier, much of the town's pride and success may be credited to the legacy created by Walt.

Residents of Marceline feel the connection to Disney in their day-to-day life. In 1960, Walt returned to Marceline to dedicate the Walt Disney Elementary School, with new art in the building's interior featuring murals of classic characters painted by Disney artists. By 2004, the town's post office had been renamed the Walt Disney US Post Office, making it the only federal building in the country named after Walt.

Marceline may not necessarily be a primary travel destination for out-of-town visitors, but its connection to Disney has brought in enough traffic to warrant the creation of the Walt Disney Hometown Museum in the Santa Fe Depot where the railroad once stopped. The barn where the Disney family farm was once located has since been rebuilt, and numerous documentaries, including *Walt, The Man Behind the Myth*, by the Walt Disney Family Foundation, have been filmed in the town.

Consider the wrought-iron details along the upper stories of Main Street's Engine Company 71 building and whether or not most comparable American towns would have such detail on a utilitarian building. Of course these details are all part of the turn-of-the-century look that Imagineers wanted to replicate when designing the park, but even such small hints of wealth may not be accurate to many American towns that Main Street is meant to remind us of. The same may be said for Disney's Hollywood Studios, where guests want to experience the Hollywood they think they know from the movies. They don't want to experience poverty, or tacky businesses trying to squeeze every last cent out of visitors for subpar tours of filming locations, or how dirty an actual functioning city can be.

The Colonial Revival Movement peaked during Walt's lifetime, likely having an unintentional impact on the designs of Main Street, U.S.A. and other areas of Disneyland and the future plans for Walt Disney World. With increasing technological advancements, Americans between about 1876 (from the centennial celebrations of the United States) to the early 1940s turned their decorative and architectural focuses back toward colonial styles. More prominent on the East Coast where most of the country's colonial architecture still stands, the movement did manage to impact architects and designers from all parts of the United States. During the Colonial Revival Movement, citizens began to create idealized architecture in their own towns. Utilitarian buildings were redesigned with new/old elements like Corinthian columns and the colors we see on Main Street, harkening back to prestigious buildings like Monticello and Mount Vernon. With the subconscious idealization of the park's designs in the minds of Walt and the Imagineers, the Main Street we see as guests in the park today is an outcome of the Colonial Revival Movement. The movement proved successful in promoting patriotism across the country, and, as Richard Francaviglia, author of *Main Street Revisited,* points out: "As people are lovingly restoring their towns, they're also filtering it through so many lenses—of memory, popular culture—that they're creating something that never actually existed before."

Speaking about Disneyland's Main Street, Walt once said, "For those of us who remember the carefree time it re-creates, Main Street will bring back happy memories. For younger visitors, it is an adventure in turning back the calendar to the days of grandfather's youth." This sense of nostalgia combined with new experiences for guests who do not have firsthand memories of a prior "Main Street" allows the park to let the aforementioned exclusions apply while still providing an authentic and memorable visit to guests who, thanks to the meticulous attention to design by Disney Imagineers, will see and remember Main Street, U.S.A. as they wish to see it.

A Tribute to Tobacco

Any smoker who visits Walt Disney World today is likely aware that tobacco is not sold in any of the theme parks. Anyone looking for a cigarette or cigar during their Disney vacation would either need to leave Disney property, or visit a merchandise location at a Disney resort (or the select few other locations like the cigar shop in Disney Springs or Mizner's Lounge at the Grand Floridian).

There was a time, however, when tobacco was not only sold in the Magic Kingdom, but in multiple locations within the park. Guests who have been coming to Disney World for the past 35 years or so may remember the tobacco shop that once existed on Main Street called the Tabacconist. The shop's former location is the spot currently occupied by the men's clothing and accessories section of the Emporium, adjacent to Casey's Corner. When the park opened, however, this was one location in the Magic Kingdom where tobacco products could be purchased.

In addition to the Tabacconist sign outside on Main Street that has long since been removed, the figure by the side of the street is left over from the shop. Across the street from where the shop was, you may come across Chief Seegar, a play on the word "cigar." Chief Seegar (and his body double that can be found in Frontierland, another location that used to sell tobacco) is an example of a cigar-store Indian.

Until the late 19th century, cigar-store Indians were popular in advertising campaigns and in displays outside of cigar shops to let passersby know the shops sold tobacco. By 1911, sidewalk regulations in many American cities and towns began to limit the size of signage and statuaries that could be out on a sidewalk for advertising purposes. Increased awareness of racial sensitivities have also played a role in the cigar-store

Indian disappearing from many towns. In addition to concerns that the figures may be seen as an insensitive caricature, some Native Americans have become frustrated that their culture's likeness has been used to sell tobacco for commercial use, where they most often use it for ceremonial purposes.

"Partners" and "Sharing the Magic"

The statues found on Main Street—*Partners* and *Sharing the Magic*—were created by Disney sculptor Blaine Gibson. Gibson began his career with Disney in 1939, when he left Colorado University due to difficulties in funding his education, to work as an assistant animator eventually credited with contributing to such films as *Fantasia*, *Bambi*, *Song of the South*, *Alice in Wonderland*, *Peter Pan*, *Sleeping Beauty*, and *One Hundred and One Dalmatians*. During his time as an animator, he took one-on-one sculpting classes at night at Pasadena City College, where he learned the skills necessary to create work for various art exhibits. It was at one such exhibit in 1954 where Walt recruited him to work in the company's newly created sculpting department that would provide many of the details in Disneyland, and later in Walt Disney World. By 1961, Gibson had become the head of that department.

By 1983, Gibson had officially retired; however, he continued to work as a consultant for various Disney projects including the Great Movie Ride which was scheduled to open with Hollywood Studios in 1989. Ten years after his retirement, the *Partners* statue, one of his most famous pieces, was unveiled in Disneyland, and has since been duplicated in many of the other Disney parks around the world.

Today, *Partners* may be seen from the hub at the end of Main Street right in front of Cinderella Castle. The statue went through numerous drafts before work on the sculpture could actually begin, as Disney Imagineers and Gibson wanted to make sure everything about Walt and Mickey's pose were just right. Among the initial ideas for the piece were poses involving a map with plans for Epcot, which did not seem as pleasing to the eye as some of the other ideas, and images of Mickey holding Walt's hand and pulling him forward, which seemed off in thinking that Walt would not be moving forward on his own. Ultimately, the way that Walt is holding Mickey's hand in the work is based on how Mickey held Leopold Stowkowski's hand while shaking it before the credits of the film *Fantasia*. More intricate details that the majority of guests will never notice from a quick glance at the statue are the inclusion of Walt's additional wedding ring, an Irish Claddagh worn on the right hand of him and his wife, Lillian, and the STR logo on his tie in reference to the Smoke Tree Ranch in Palm Springs where Walt often vacationed.

The statue was originally planned as being specific to Disneyland, but another was created for Walt Disney World's Magic Kingdom just two years later, in 1995, with the only difference being a slight change in color to better compliment the different style of the Florida park. Blaine's other contribution to Main Street U.S.A. is specific to the Magic Kingdom however, and may be found in the circular area by the flag pole closer to the train station and park entrance.

Sharing the Magic is Gibson's bronze statue depicting Roy Disney and Minnie Mouse holding hands while seated on a bench. Following Walt's death in 1966, his brother Roy took it upon himself to continue the development of Walt Disney World (then the Florida Project). *Sharing the Magic* was originally placed in a different location on Main Street behind a fence, but so many guests attempted to climb over the fence to sit with Roy and Minnie that the company decided to move the piece to a more public area.

The statue's current location is no accident. It may be seen (or sat next to) where Roy Disney gave his dedication speech for the park on opening day, October 1, 1971. The statue Gibson created symbolizes Roy's role in the creation of the resort by the way he is holding Minnie's hand. Roy's hand is placed underneath Minnie's, as if to be holding her up or supporting her—the same way that Roy would have supported Walt with his dreams of creating magical lands that may have seemed impossible to others at the time.

Another noteworthy characteristic of body language is the position of Roy sitting farther back into the bench with Minnie leaning forward. Gibson based the design of the statue on photographs of Roy sitting with characters during the year the park opened, and in the piece he wanted to imply that Roy was on the bench first and that Minnie came to him, and not that "he came up to her to ask why she was sitting down and not working," Gibson has humorously explained. Today many guests sit next to Minnie for photos, which does make for a fun photo op, though this was not Blaine's intention in leaving a space on the bench next to Minnie. For Roy being such an important figure in the creation of Disney World, but also someone who was often seen in the shadow of his brother Walt, Gibson wanted Minnie to appear sitting close and leaning into Roy to make him seem as approachable as he was in real life, even if he spent much of his work on the park behind the scenes and away from the public eye.

Completed for the Walt Disney World Resort in 1999, when Gibson had long been retired (and was 81 years old), *Sharing the Magic* is the first piece of his that most guests experience when arriving to spend a day in the Magic Kingdom.

Inspiration in Film

So far, we've noted that Main Street, U.S.A. has been based on concepts from Marceline, Missouri, the 1893 Chicago World's Fair, Colonial Revivalism, and even the writing of a famous American poet, but inspiration has also been found in film. The most obvious American film reference on Main Street can be found at Tony's Town Square, a restaurant based on the famous spaghetti-and-meatball scene from *Lady and the Tramp*. And the setting of the film itself is even said to be based on Marceline, Missouri. Sound familiar?

Tony's Town Square was not always themed to *Lady and the Tramp*. The restaurant was known as the Town Square Café when the park opened, and it was originally sponsored by Oscar Mayer. The décor of the café followed suit with the rest of Main Street using the beige and pastel color scheme with Victorian details. Ironically enough, the original restaurant featured a wide variety of menu items including fried catfish and Monte Cristo sandwiches, before converting to an American-Italian eatery when it was converted to Tony's Town Square in 1989.

Walt Disney World's Main Street also features nods to a lesser-known live-action Disney musical from 1963: *Summer*

Magic, a turn-of-the-century musical which follows a Boston widow who moves to a small town in Maine with her children. The name "Osh Popham" is displayed as the proprietor by one of the windows near the Emporium, a reference to Osh Popham the shopkeeper in the film, and singer of the song "Ugly Bug Ball." (Although this song saw a seemingly random spurt of popularity in the United Kingdom, it was never particularly popular in the United States. If you grew up in the 90s, however, you may recognize it from one of the old straight-to-VHS Disney sing-along films.) Osh Popham in the film is played by Burl Ives, who is also known for his portrayal of Sam the Snowman in the classic Christmas film *Rudolph the Red-Nosed Reindeer*. Despite Ives proving himself as a talented actor, he was largely ostracized by the entertainment community at various points throughout his career (but primarily during the 1950s) due to pursuing Communist ties in his relationships.

Le Chapeau, or the hat shop, on Main Street has an address listed outside as No. 63, a reference to the year the film was released. Le Chapeau was also originally intended (per the building's storyline) to be run by characters from the film, Nancy and Julia Carey. Though the signage bearing their names has since been removed, the silhouettes seen on the walls inside the shop may be of the two girls.

Music on Main Street

No discussion of Main Street would be complete without mentioning the area's music. As a fully immersive experience, music has an important role in transporting guests to different times and places across Walt Disney World. Wearing headphones with today's music pouring into your ears can easily take you right out of that turn-of-the-century, Victorian feel that you are meant to experience while strolling down Main Street. (Of course, some might argue that visiting Starbucks would have the same effect, but that's a debate for another time.)

Main Street primarily uses ragtime music, which was prevalent in the United States from the 1890s to about 1915. Though ragtime became quite popular across the entire country, music historians believe that the style originated in the Midwest, and most likely in Missouri. Like most forms of music, ragtime styles varied based on the part of the country new songs were originating from, but the Library of Congress defines the style as "a genre of musical composition for the piano, generally in duple meter and containing a highly syncopated treble lead over a rhythmically steady bass. A ragtime composition is usually composed od three or four contrasting sections or strains, each one being 16 or 32 measures in length."

The upbeat syncopation characteristic of ragtime is commonly heard in musicals based on this time period, and it even caused an increase in piano sales in the United States that lasted right up to the start of the 1920s. Guests on Main Street can get a taste for the music performed live on a piano at Casey's Corner at varying intervals from about noon to 6:00 pm (depending on the specific daily schedule). One of the cast members guests may spot as a pianist at Casey's is Jim Omohundro, who has been playing at the classic hot dog spot since Thanksgiving Day, 1983. Jim is also the recipient of the Disney Legacy Award, the highest honor any cast member in the company can receive, and is noted by the blue nametags worn in contrast to the usual white ones.

Many of the specific songs played on Main Street come from classic musicals, or are simply well-known piano tunes that most guests have probably heard at one time or another. A couple of the songs that have been heard on Main Street over the years including "Flitterin" and "Summer Magic" which were originally used in the film *Summer Magic*, and were written by the Sherman Brothers. Other songs authentic to the time period include 1912's "It's a Long Way to Tipperary," which was initially known for being sung by British soldiers in World War I before it gained popularity in the United States, and "Meet Me in St. Louis," which serves as a reference for the 1904 St. Louis World's Fair.

While most of the songs are within the time period on Main Street, the song "Put on Your Sunday Clothes" was revived in popularity when it was showcased in a scene in the beginning of the film *WALL-E*, though it was originally featured in the 1964 musical *Hello, Dolly!* The most modern song heard on Main Street is "Married Life," the instrumental (and ultimately tear-jerking) tune from the opening sequences of *Up!* Other notable songs include features from the 1957 musical *The Music Man*. Main Street's most recent musical changes were recorded in Capitol Studios by Dean Mora's Ragtime Orchestra, and included both original songs with ragtime-style updates to newer songs to help them better fit the turn-of-the-century theme.

In addition to the music piped into Main Street (through speakers often hidden behind what appear to be vents in the buildings), there are live musical offerings that fit right in with the time period of the area as well. Two to three times per day, guests are also treated to more music from this period thanks to the brass and percussion sounds of the Main Street Philharmonic.

Main Street's very own barbershop quartet, the Dapper Dans, perform for guests daily in the morning and afternoon. Barbershop quartets, which consist of four singers (tenor, lead, baritone, and bass) were popular in the late 19th and early 20th centuries, though their popularity faded as the "newer" music of the 1920s became more prominent. Walt Disney's love for barbershop quartet style music grew in the years immediately following the opening of Disneyland. He enjoyed the music so much that he called upon the popular quartet, the Mellomen, to record *Meet Me Down on Main Street,* an album that was fittingly sold in the park upon its debut in 1957. The Dapper Dans as we know them today have been a staple on Disneyland's Main Street since the late 1950s, and at Disney World since the park's opening in 1971.

Wondering what those strange-looking instruments that the Dapper Dans usually play are? They are called Deagan organ chimes, a vaudeville-style instrument patented in 1900 in Chicago by the chimes' namesake, John Calhoun Deagan. Deagan's manufacturing company eventually became responsible for the production of many of the United States' xylophones, tuba bells, church bells, cowbells, and rattles throughout the 20th century. The Dapper Dans in Disneyland prior to 1971 did not use any chimes in their performances; their sets consisted only of the quartet singing and tap dancing. It was not until Disney World's first set of Dapper Dans began performing in 1971 that the Deagan organ chimes were introduced. One of the Magic Kingdom's original Dan's, Charles David "Bub" Thomas, had used the chimes in his previous positions in other barbershop quartets, and it was his suggestion to use them that brought the chimes to Disney World.

Thomas had years of experience in the vaudeville circuit and was a talented performer in multiple bands and barbershop quartets before a friend suggested that he try out for the position in the new Disney World group. He then joined the opening cast of the Dapper Dans, where he stayed with the group performing on Main Street for guests for just over 25 years. While many regular guests to the park are familiar with the 12+ performers that rotate through the roles of the Dapper Dans, Thomas created special memories for many guests by sketching them cartoons and mailing them as souvenirs. Remembered as one of Main Street's greatest cast members, Thomas died in a car accident in 1997 at the age of 85. A tribute to Thomas and the rest of the park's original Dapper Dans may be found in a sketch of the foursome that is hanging on a wall inside the Harmony Barber Shop.

Walt Disney World Railroad

The Walt Disney World Railroad, with stops at the entrance to Main Street, Frontierland, and Fantasyland, brings guests back in time to the age of the great steam trains. The attraction is a tribute to Walt Disney and his love for locomotives. Walt's interest in trains began early in his life while he and his family were still residing in Marceline. Though most known for providing the inspiration for Main Street, Marceline is a true railroad town. The town grew around the railroad station there in 1888, when it began to serve as a crossroads for the Atchison, Topeka, and Santa Fe Railways. The trains not only sparked an interest in Walt because of their technological awe, but also because his uncle worked as an engineer on them. His uncle Mike would often stop in Marceline to visit with the family when his route required a layover there, and during these times would describe his life on the rails. Walt was always thrilled to learn more about what working on the trains was like, and he eagerly awaited the days when his uncle would be in town.

Influenced by his uncle, young Walt dreamed of being an engineer one day. He had spent so much time in Marceline watching trains come and go, and reading the various locations on the side of the cars dreaming of the adventures that would take place traveling to distant locations by rail. While still in Marceline, Walt did manage to work on the railroad, though not as an engineer as he was still under 10 years old at the time. Walt followed in his brother Roy's footsteps and became a news butcher for a Missouri Pacific commuter train that ran between Kansas City and Jefferson City. A job that really is not around much anymore, at least in the United States, a news butcher was a person, usually a young boy, who would walk up and down the dining cars on lower end or commuter trains selling everything from light refreshments to tobacco, and of course the newspaper. It was not a glamorous job by any means, but for a boy with a thirst for adventure on the rails it would have been exhilarating.

Another connection between Walt and the railroad is often made when considering how Mickey Mouse was created. According to tradition, Walt sketched Mickey while on a train from New York to Los Angeles, after having realized that he did not own the rights to his Oswald character, which would remain part of Universal for a number of years. He then sketched a mouse character, which he elected to name Mortimer until his wife Lillian expressed her disdain for the name Mortimer and suggested Mickey instead.

While the basic premise of this story is true, the actual events that led to the creation of Mickey are unclear. Walt himself retold the story in a variety of different ways over the years, as did his wife, and at one point his nephew Roy E. Disney even pointed out that we don't really know when exactly Mickey was created. Whether the idea for Mickey came to Walt on the train ride, or shortly after his arrival in Los Angeles, it seems safe to say that the train ride did have a lasting impact on Walt's memory as he often mentioned it when retelling the story.

By 1950, following a series ups and downs (with international revenue being down in the 1940s as a result of World War II), Walt was finally able to achieve his dream of building his very own railroad…in his backyard.

Walt recognized the need for something to do just for fun around his studio, and so following a polo injury he decided to put a model train set in the room next to his office. Lionel Trains had a working relationship with Walt, and even sponsored the parts for his model train. Soon after Walt was finished with the train, interest around the studio grew, primarily with animator Ward Kimball. Another animator who showed a great interest in the trains in Walt's office was Ollie Johnston. Walt had one more personal influencer on his love of trains at the studio: Hazel George, the studio nurse, who after continuing to see Walt struggle through his recovery from his polo injury, suggested that he visit the Chicago Railroad Fair as a way of relieving his stress.

Following that advice, Walt invited Kimball to come along and the two went off to the fair in Chicago. The Chicago Museum of Science and Industry was responsible for the organization of the event, which featured exhibits from present-day railroad giants as well as locomotives and their history of the past. The trip to Chicago provided the much-needed relaxation that Walt needed, and it allowed him to put work aside, even if only for a few days, to have some fun.

Shortly after his return to the studio, Walt began expressing interest in creating a theme park, then just referred to as a "Mickey Mouse Park," and he insisted that it would be "like nothing else in the world, and it should be surrounded by a train." This was about the time when Walt enlisted the studio's chief mechanic (as well as train enthusiast and future Imagineer), Roger Broggie, to work on the Carolwood Pacific, a 1/8 scale railroad that would serve as the model for the Disneyland Railroad and later as the inspiration for the Disney World Railroad.

The Carolwood Pacific would eventually become a live steam locomotive covering just over 2,600 feet of track in Walt's own back yard. When the plans were laid for the train, Walt faced opposition from his wife, Lillian, who did not want her backyard to become a railroad, and did not want to lose her flowerbeds to feet of track. Walt strategically came up with every possible alternative in the train's design to avoid upsetting his wife, and he ultimately changed the name of the locomotive from the original No. 173 to the *Lilly Belle*, a name that honored his wife and would later be carried over to his theme parks.

The Walt Disney World Railroad is made up of four trains: *Walter E. Disney, Lilly Belle, Roy O. Disney,* and *Roger E. Broggie.* These locomotives are authentic vintage pieces that were manufactured between 1916 and 1928 by the Baldwin Locomotive Works in Philadelphia. They were originally used on the Ferrocarriles Unidos de Yucatan where they carried jute, sugar, hemp, and passengers through the southeastern jungles of Mexico. The trains carried out this purpose for a number of years before they were found in Merida, Mexico, nearing the end of their lifespans, by Disney executives in 1969. Roger Broggie led the search for the steam engines, and opted to purchase five of the antique trains for a sum of $32,750. Though five trains were initially purchased, only four exist in the Magic Kingdom today as one was found to be too far past repairing to justify the restoration.

The renovations to the trains took place in Tampa, Florida, wherein each locomotive was updated and restored with new smokestacks, steam whistles, cowcatchers, boiler jackets, and headlamps, and of course the signature paint scheme that we see on the trains today. The passenger coaches within the trains were also rebuilt from scratch during the restoration, while the wheels and side rods are all original parts.

While steam trains were already prevalent in other countries, the United States did not fully embrace rail travel until about 1830, and the two American coasts were not linked by the Transcontinental Railroad until 1869. The Transcontinental Railroad was a standard gauge system; the narrow gauge railroads that we tend to see more of today run on narrower tracks, and therefore require smaller locomotives that are less expensive to build. Though the Walt Disney World Railroad would be considered narrow gauge, the land around the parks is not as flat as we may imagine, and so these locomotives have to deal with grades of up to 2%.

As the locomotives in the parks are all steam engines, a water pumping system is necessary to constantly turn the supply of incoming water into steam. Though simpler and more modern methods of converting water to steam have been devised in recent years, the Magic Kingdom trains still use the classical method of pumping water from a tender tank into a boiler while movement is already taking place.

Three of the Walt Disney World locomotives, the *Walter E. Disney*, *Roger E. Broggie*, and *The Lilly Belle*, all feature diamond stack smokestacks. The name "diamond stack" refers to the diamond-like shape seen at the top of the train's exhaust stack. The diamond stack was created to keep hot cinders from leaving through the exhaust. In the early days of the steam engines, problems persisted where hot cinders would leave with the smoke out of the exhaust, causing danger to farmland the trains would pass should a piece of cinder set the land ablaze. The diamond stack is fitted with a series of screens on the interior to filter out any materials that are not steam and keep them from escaping through the exhaust.

The *Walter E. Disney* and the *Roger E. Broggie* were both manufactured in 1925, and are the types of locomotives known as ten-wheelers. They use the configuration of 4-6-0, or 4 wheels by the front of the engine, 6 in the middle, and 0 by the rear. The *Lilly Belle*, the newest of the Walt Disney World trains, was manufactured in 1928 and uses a 2-6-0 configuration, with 2 wheels by the engine, 6 in the middle, and 0 in the rear. The *Lilly Belle's* passenger cabin includes one additional accommodation in terms of the size and access from certain cars: this train has been used to open the park when the morning welcome show took place at the train station, and as such needed to be fitted for characters to be able to safely and quickly get on and off the car.

The *Roy O. Disney* is the oldest locomotive at Walt Disney World, having been manufactured in 1916. It also features the unique wheel configuration of 2-4-2, making it the only train in the Magic Kingdom with wheels in the rear. Additionally, *Roy O. Disney* features a balloon stack rather than a diamond stack above the exhaust. Balloon stacks were common with earlier locomotives that ran on coal or wood burning, but could later be fitted to essentially have the same function as a diamond stack in catching hot cinders from leaving the exhaust.

Next time you visit the Walt Disney World Railroad (at the Main Street Station) spend some time looking at the artwork and various artifacts that can be found throughout the station. The station itself is inspired by ones of the same era found in Saratoga Springs, New York, and there are plenty of beautiful Victorian details to take in while walking through the station. In the tunnel below the station, you can find framed paperwork with information behind the namesakes for each of the trains, along with maps of the railways present at the turn of the century. On the upper level, classic arcade games that originally existed in the penny arcade may be viewed, along with some Disney-created paintings of historical rail events. One such device is the mutoscope, or a machine that projects a moving picture when guests look through the class and manually crank the device. The mutoscope labeled "Old San Francisco" is connected to modern-day pop culture through one of the actresses featured. The projection shows Delores Costello, the grandmother of actress Drew Barrymore. There are six mutoscopes in the train station, and they serve as entertaining and unique artifacts from a simpler time.

CHAPTER 2

Liberty Square

From Liberty Street to Liberty Square

Past this gateway stirs a new nation waiting to be born. Thirteen separate colonies have banded together to declare their independence from the bonds of tyranny. It is a time when silversmiths put away their tools and march to the drums of a revolution, a time when gentleman planters leave their farms to become generals, a time when tradesmen leave the safety of home to become heroes. Welcome to Liberty Square!

These words are engraved on the plaque that guests encounter on their way into Liberty Square from the hub in front of Cinderella Castle. While vague in detail, they embody the vision that Walt Disney had for including an American Revolution-themed area in Disneyland called Liberty Street that never came to fruition. Liberty Square is based largely on Walt's original ideas for Liberty Street, a colonial land that would have existed off a side street of Main Street in Disneyland. In entering Liberty Street, guests would have walked a cobblestone road, passing shops selling authentic 18th century wares, and experiencing full immersion in the time period. By the time of Walt's death, Liberty Street still had not yet become more than a concept, and Imagineers took it upon themselves to move the idea to the Florida and add it to the Magic Kingdom.

The American Revolution is one of the most misunderstood time periods in American history, not because Americans do not necessarily know all of the details of the event, but because when most of us learn about it much of the information is glossed over. Most Americans grow up with the broad understanding of the fight for independence that we learn in grade school, which at a most basic level can be broken down into: 1. Britain taxes the colonies without their consent; 2. The colonists unanimously (or at least almost unanimously) agree that this is wrong, and they should fight for independence; and 3. The colonists win (clearly) because today the United States is not a part of Great Britain.

Aside from the smaller details regarding how these taxes actually worked, what Disney (and an alarming number of other Revolutionary-era tourist attractions) fail to convey to guests is that the desire for independence was not even close to unanimous. The colonies had their fair share of Loyalists, who viewed their Patriot counterparts as subjects of the crown who were committing treason against their country. Then there are the smaller details that Liberty Square gets wrong that most guests probably do not think of. Although not meant to be the most educational display of the American Revolution, Great Moments in History with the Muppets gets the story of Paul Revere wrong, implying that the silversmith was never captured and that he was not accompanied by other riders. Another crude inaccuracy is the Christmas store which would have been out of place in Revolutionary-era America.

The Hall of Presidents: A Celebration of Liberty's Leaders

Had Liberty Street ever been created, Walt planned for a show that would later be reworked into what we see today as the Hall of Presidents, then conceived as "One Nation Under God." This show would have worked very similarly to the Hall of Presidents, using a circular film to display paintings and photos from landmark events throughout American history, with a finale starring figures of all the country's presidents. One Nation Under God was ultimately cancelled because the technology to make the figures of the presidents look and work as Walt and the Imagineers would have wanted was not yet there.

The Hall of Presidents took the concept of Disneyland's Great Moments with Mr. Lincoln along with the planned One Nation Under God show and ran with it, creating one of the most elaborate displays of audio-animatronic shows available anywhere. The show opened with the park in 1971, featuring animatronics originally sculpted by Blaine Gibson, who did the work on the bronze statues on Main Street of Walt and Roy. After Gibson sculpted his final president, George W. Bush, Valerie Edwards took over for the design of President Obama's animatronic. In addition to the Hall of Presidents, Edwards worked on the refurbishment of the Pirates of the Caribbean attraction that introduced Captain Jack Sparrow and Barbossa.

The interior pre-show space was not added to the attraction until 1973. Today it allows guests to view an exhibit featuring items (both authentic and replicas) that once belonged to presidents and their wives. Because the original show focused on the importance of the Constitution, the year 1787 may be seen outside on the building's façade in reference to the year that the Constitution was signed.

The first then-current president to be included in the show was Richard Nixon, as he was the sitting president when the park opened in 1971. Nixon did not have a speaking role in the attraction as the current president, though he was the focus of the show during the finale scene with many anxious guests curious about seeing a living president in animatronic form. The first current president to speak in the attraction was Bill Clinton, who was added to the show in 1993. During this version of the show, the script was nearly entirely re-written by Eric Foner, a professor from Columbia University. Foner was able to successfully convince Michael Eisner that the script for the Hall of Presidents needed some work to be more historically accurate, and to be more inclusive of topics that had traditionally been left out like ethical and civil problems through the country's history including slavery.

Eisner took Foner up on his offer, and a new, more rounded script was introduced into the show. In reworking the show's narration, Foner updated Lincoln's speech which had been close to his original speech in Disneyland's Great Moments with Mr. Lincoln, and he also wrote the speech that Clinton recited when the show reopened during his presidency. The newer version of the show marked a departure from the days of the original show where internal Disney cast provided the narration, as narrators from then on would include accomplished American celebrities like Maya Angelou, J.D. Hall, and Morgan Freeman.

The accuracy of the show was further improved in 2006, when Disney recruited presidential historian Doris Kearns Goodwin to update various aspects of the show. Included in her update were changes to some of the wardrobes of the presidents, and extensive research that went into the film portion of the presentation.

In addition to the speech written by his speechwriter, Jon Favreau, Obama's version of the show also featured him taking the oath of office. Ironically enough, the recording of Obama's speech and the oath of office were both done in the White House Map Room. This was the same room in the White House where Obama re-took the oath of office following his inauguration, as Chief Justice John Roberts, who had delivered the initial oath, stumbled on some of the words, causing the president to do the same. Prior to recording his speech, when Disney Imagineers showed Obama the rendering of his animatronic thus far, he humorously commented that they had made him better looking than in real life.

The Hall of Presidents is one of many instances in Walt Disney World where the level of detail is so high that much of the audience may never even notice the amount of work that went into the design. The clothing that each of the presidents wear in the show, for instance, is extremely accurate to their time periods. Imagineers went so far as to seek out the same types of fabrics used to create authentic outfits, which guests will likely never notice from the distance of the seating area. They even went so far as to re-create Obama's wedding ring. (The one notable inaccuracy in appearance would be George Washington's hair. While powdered wigs were common during the time period, Washington actually powdered his own hair, meaning that his hair in the show should have a slight reddish hue rather than the full white color we see on the animatronic.) Another incredible detail comes with President Franklin D. Roosevelt, who even though the audience cannot see it, wears polio braces under his pant legs.

A more noticeable detail that guests usually notice as soon as they enter the pre-show area is the Great Seal of the United

States woven into the rug in the center of the room. The only other place that displays the Great Seal is the White House, and Disney had to get permission through an Act of Congress to display the seal in the attraction.

The one major issue I see (and presumably others have noticed too with the Hall of Presidents) is the interpretation of Andrew Jackson featured in the show. The basis for including Jackson as one of the show's standout presidents is that he was "one of us." Whereas the other presidents featured came from wealthy backgrounds, Andrew Jackson was not a member of the aristocracy prior to becoming president.

So far, so good. The show does, however, gloss over or rather avoid altogether some of the more infamous practices that took place under Jackson's presidency. For one, Jackson had long been a self-proclaimed advocate for "Indian removal," eventually signing the Indian Removal Act during his presidency in 1830. The act gave the federal government the ability to swap desirable native-occupied land for land in what was referred to as the Indian colonization zone in what would be present-day Oklahoma. This process resulted in one of the most upsetting moments in American history: the Trail of Tears. In addition to the estimated 5,000 Native American lives lost as a result of the Trail of Tears, and the infinite numbers of displaced peoples when their new "home" became a state and they were pushed farther away, many historians take issue with other Jacksonian practices including the spoils system and his treatment of the National Bank.

The Hall of Presidents is a particularly tricky situation where it becomes difficult to decipher controversial moments in American history. As we see during every presidential election season, everyone has different views of what is right and wrong, and what makes a competent leader. Especially with recent presidents, it is difficult to make a case for or against their role in the attraction. President Trump's inclusion in the Hall of Presidents has proved to be controversial among guests. It marks the longest time that the attraction has been closed while Imagineers add the current president's animatronic, and it is the first time that the park has assigned security cast members in both the preshow area and in the main theatre.

Christmas Who?

Ye Olde Christmas Shoppe, located directly across from the Hall of Presidents, is not something that would have existed around the time of the Revolutionary War. Even assuming that the timeframe of Liberty Square is later than the area's welcome sign would suggest (given that the Hall of Presidents has the year 1787, when the Constitution was adopted, inscribed on the building), it is unlikely that most Americans were celebrating Christmas during this time.

The Puritan religion, which was the most prevalent religion through the end of the 18th century, did not celebrate Christmas at all, and most historians agree that Christmas was brought later to the United States by German immigrants and other groups of Europeans. In fact, earlier Puritans outlawed the celebration of Christmas altogether for some time. In Boston, for instance, celebrating Christmas was a crime between 1659 and 1681, and colonists who were caught doing so would be required to pay a fine of 5 shillings.

Puritans focused their beliefs primarily on scripture, which they felt said nothing in the way of a celebration being necessary for Christmas. Instead, most Puritans continued to work and go about their day-to-day lives during the Christmas season, without celebrating at all, as recognizing the holiday was a practice they would have associated with paganism. Though Christmas celebrations were made legal by the end of the 17th century, most early Americans still did not celebrate, and the day was not granted federal holiday status until 1870.

There is a loosely understood story that the Christmas shop is run by the Kepples, a German family of craftsmen. The name Kepple is a reference to Walt's grandfather, Kepple Disney, and a sign with his name exists outside of the shop. Though this may be one official explanation for the Christmas shop existing in Liberty Square, it is not adequate considering that a German family operating a Christmas shop in the colonies still would have been unlikely.

Since Christmas was not a widely celebrated holiday in the colonies during Liberty Square's respective time frame, there are a couple of other possible reasons for Disney's inclusion of Ye

Olde Christmas Shoppe in Liberty Square. One may be simply that Christmas ornaments are popular tourist souvenirs, and including a shop for these items in the Magic Kingdom makes sense from a business standpoint. Thematically, it would make even less sense to have the shop located in Adventureland, Frontierland, Fantasyland, or Tomorrowland, although Main Street may have been more logical than Liberty Square. The only other reason (and this may be a stretch) is that although the colonists did not celebrate Christmas, the dates of Christmas Eve and Christmas Day were actually important in terms of the Revolution, so Ye Olde Christmas Shoppe may be the ultimate Easter egg of hidden inspiration in Liberty Square. It is doubtful that a convoluted connection to an event that took place during Christmas is the reason for the shop; however, this instance is the only true historical connection to the theme of Liberty Square.

Some historians believe that Hessian soldiers (German troops hired by the British to fight during the Revolution) brought the practice of Christmas to the United States, while others believe that the tradition did not become prevalent until some time later when waves of German immigrants settled in eastern Pennsylvania.

The colonists may not have celebrated Christmas during the Revolution, but the Hessian troops did. George Washington's famous crossing of the Delaware River with over 2,000 troops was planned as a surprise attack on the Hessians who were just finishing up their Christmas festivities. Washington and his troops were able to surround the Hessians the following morning on December 26, 1776, when they were exhausted (and likely hungover) from celebrating the night before, and were able to capture 1,000 Hessian soldiers with only four of Washington's soldiers lost. In the grand scheme of strategic battles in the American Revolution, this event may not be the most memorable. In fact, the famous painting depicting Washington and his troops crossing the Delaware by Emanuel Leutze may even be more known to Americans today than the actual event itself. It is, however, one of two instances that may be the reason for the seemingly random reference to Christmas in a land that theoretically should not be celebrating the holiday at all (or selling ornaments from it).

The other event taking place close to Christmas in this time period would be December 23, 1783, when Washington announced to Congress that he would be stepping down as commander-in-chief of the Continental Army. In his formal announcement, Washington explained that with the signing of the Treaty of Paris, and the battle for independence successfully fought, he would be retiring to his home at Mount Vernon. As we know, in just five years Washington would be elected unanimously as the first president of the United States, stepping down from that office after two terms and so rejecting the concept of kingship in favor of a greater democracy.

Using either of these events as a rationale to explain the inclusion of Ye Olde Christmas Shoppe in Liberty Square may seem a bit far-fetched (because it is). With Christmas having no logical place in a Revolutionary colony, these events serve as the only real notable connections to the holiday, given the theme and time period.

The official story of the Christmas shop begins with understanding the shops that previously occupied the site: a parfumerie, silversmith shop, and an antiques shop. Open from 1972 to 1996, Olde World Antiques sold authentic antiques and reproduction items that much more closely fit the theme of Liberty Square. Though Disney has never given an official reason for this store's closure, one widely accepted belief is that selling authentic antiques in a theme park was not the most cost-effective way of running a store. With so many one-of-a-kind items, a lot of effort would have gone into purchasing them in the first place, only to resell them for a meager profit assuming most guests were not necessarily looking to take home expensive (and potentially breakable and irreplaceable) goods while visiting the Magic Kingdom.

Mademoiselle Lafayette's Parfumerie, was a unique shopping experience in that it was one of only four locations in the country where guests could create their own custom blends of perfume. Merchandise cast members were even able to keep records of each guests' blends so they would be able to come back and purchase more of each scent once they ran out.

The silversmith shop, as you would imagine, sold silver souvenirs similar to what you may see at gift shops in places like Colonial Williamsburg, Philadelphia, or Boston's Freedom Trail today. Though it is believed that the shop was inspired by Johnny Tremaine, of the Disney film, and the Esther Forbes book of the same title, it may have also been inspired by another well-known silversmith, Paul Revere.

Officially, the Christmas shop is meant to fit into the theme of Liberty Square under the assumption that since the Revolutionary War was over (at least at the Christmas shop) and Americans were then free to practice whatever religion they would like, a modest Christmas shop would exist to sell holiday wares. The style of the Christmas shop then follows the style of the three separate shops that had been the building's previous tenants, with each section housing a different kind of Christmas merchandise.

Smile from the Stocks!

Another tell-tale sign of Liberty Square essentially functioning as a tourist attraction is the placement of the pillory in the land's center. A pillory only restricts the person's arms and head, while stocks also fit around the person's feet making them unable to move their legs. Liberty Square's most touristy photo op therefore features a pillory.

Pillories are authentic to colonial towns, but they are often placed in history-based tourist attractions with little or no explanation for how they were actually used. Mostly they are used for goofy photos of the family smiling while having their head and arms restrained in the openings. Pillories were common in colonial towns as they were used in punishments for crimes that called for public humiliation. While it should come as no surprise that the people stuck in a pillory were criminals, it may be shocking to think about the sorts of "crimes" that would result in this kind of punishment.

Throughout New England, many colonists who ended up in the pillory (or the stocks) did so because they failed to attend church. Before there was a separation of church and state, and during the height of the Puritan religion in the region, colonists could be punished for missing church services on a repeated basis. Many communities operated similarly to how small American towns function today in that everyone tends to know everyone else's business. If you weren't in church for a couple of services in a row, somebody was bound to notice, and if caught you may find yourself serving time in the town pillory.

Another crime that could land a person in the pillory would be public drunkenness. Colonists were expected to lead good, moral lives, and public intoxication was viewed as a hefty crime. In some colonies, swearing was against the law, and depending on how the local government operated one could find themselves in the pillory for using some choice words in public. Behaving in a way that was considered "inappropriate" with the opposite gender was also reason for public humiliation.

Once in the stocks or the pillory, for whatever amount of time was determined based on the crime, the other people in the town would sometimes join in on the punishment. The person who committed the crime would not only be locked in the wooden frame for all to see, but the other colonists would occasionally make the punishment worse by throwing rocks or rotten fruit at the criminal. In today's terms, many of the crimes that would have led one to the pillory in the 18th century seem to not warrant such a punishment. During this time period, however, the pillory was likely one of the "better" punishments a person could hope for when being accused of committing a crime. Worse than the pillory would be a trip to the whipping post, brandings, or hangings, all of which would be done in a public area like the town common. It is ironic that what was once used as a form of brutal punishment about 300 years ago is presently used as a silly photo spot.

All About the Details

Some references to the design of Liberty Square indicate that the bridge guests cross over when entering the land from the hub is meant to represent the Old North Bridge in Concord, Massachusetts, where the first battle of the American Revolution took place. While this may have been the original intention of the bridge, there is nothing in the immediate area that suggests that the bridge is based on this one specific bridge, nor does the bridge look all that similar to the original Old North Bridge. If your imagination allows you to believe that you are walking across the Concord River on such a historic bridge, there is no concrete evidence suggesting the bridge's true influence one way or another. However, if you have such a desire to cross the *real* Old North Bridge, you'll need to plan a visit to Concord, Massachusetts, where guests are able to visit the bridge as part of the Minuteman National Historical Park.

Following suit with the typical Revolutionary town, Liberty Square is also home to a Liberty Tree. The original Liberty Tree was an elm located in Boston on an outskirt of Boston Common. This Liberty Tree is no longer standing in Boston, but if you are looking for its former location, you'll want to visit the intersection of Washington and Essex Street, where the building currently at 630 Washington Street has a plaque marking the original site. In Boston, the Sons of Liberty famously met under the branches of the tree to protest the Stamp Act in 1765, prompting other colonists to do the same in their towns.

Walt Disney World's Liberty Tree has been located in the heart of Liberty Square since the park opened, and today it is the oldest tree in the Magic Kingdom. The tree, a 100+ year old southern live oak, was moved from another location on Disney World property only about eight miles from where it currently stands. While most trees can be pulled up out of the ground and moved using a cable, doing so for this tree would have been impossible. Its root ball measured 18 feet by 16 feet and was about four feet deep and the tree itself weighed close to 35 tons. Bill Evans, the head of the landscaping department for the Magic Kingdom, devised a method where holes would be drilled straight through the tree with steel rods inserted that could be used to hoist the tree out of the ground without damaging it. The tree was lowered into its present location using a 100-ton crane.

This method of moving the tree almost went off completely without a hitch, until it was discovered that some rot had developed where the holes drilled, which have since been filled with cement to prevent the rot from spreading throughout the tree. In the early 1970s, the damage in the bark near the base of the tree from where some of the holes were drilled used to be visible, though the bark has since healed over much of the damage, and the bushes have grown around it over time. The tree is decorated with 13 lanterns, representative of the 13 original colonies.

Nearby, guests will also see a replica of the Liberty Bell that was cast from the same mold as the original for Disney World in 1989. The original Liberty Bell has been property of the National Park Service since 1948, and it sits in a glass pavilion within the NPS Visitor Center in Philadelphia. The first replica of the Liberty Bell at the Magic Kingdom was showcased in the park during the bicentennial celebrations of the U.S. Constitution. The bell proved to be as popular a photo op with guests as the pillory, and it was decided that the bell would become a permanent part of Liberty Square. This particular bell however was loaned to the company from the Mount Vernon Memorial Park and Mortuary in Fair Oaks, California. When the bell was returned, Disney commissioned a new replica to be cast for the park, which was made at the Paccard Fonderie of Annecy, France, using the original mold.

The flags that create a circle around the Liberty Bell today were once located by the bridge at the entrance to Liberty Square by the hub. They each represent one of the 13 colonies, and the brass plaques at the bases of each flag pole display the dates that the states ratified the Constitution.

Liberty Square is full of small details that reference the history of the period. The two lanterns in a window above the Hall of Presidents, for instance, are a nod to the "Midnight Ride of Paul Revere" poem by Henry Wadsworth Longfellow, in which the poet wrote, "One if by land, two if by sea" (regarding how the British soldiers were arriving prior to Revere's fateful ride).

If you have ever noticed that the window shutters on the buildings in Liberty Square appear to be hanging crooked, this part of the design is actually intentional. The shutters used to be fastened with leather, which would wear over time cause them to lose their symmetrical appearance and become crooked. The crooked shutters on the buildings in Liberty Square are actually hanging by metal that is distressed to resemble leather.

Another such detail is the coloring of the concrete, with a brown line running down the center of the streets. This line is a reference to the rudimentary sewage disposal system in the 18th century, where chamber pots were used in place of modern restrooms, and their contents were tossed out into the streets. The strangest authenticity in Liberty Square then is the fact that there are no public restrooms. The restrooms at the Liberty Tree Tavern are reserved for guests dining there, and the restrooms in Columbia Harbour House are technically located in Fantasyland. To find the nearest restrooms in Liberty Square, guests can follow the brown trail in the road which will bring them out of Liberty Square toward a restroom.

Columbia Harbour House is the only instance of a building existing in two lands. The restaurant is portrayed as being part of Liberty Square, though part of the building sits geographically in Fantasyland, which is justified by the story of the site being that of two harbors—one in England (Fantasyland) and one in the American colonies (Liberty Square). The Fantasyland side of the building also has an entirely different style, one that may seem more appropriate to Germany in World Showcase than to anything in the Magic Kingdom. The later and more European style is used in the building's design to ease the transition between the two lands. The name "Columbia" is a reference to the sailing ship *Columbia* which in 1787 became the first American ship to circumnavigate the globe.

The riverboat in Liberty Square sails the Rivers of America from the dock to around Tom Sawyer Island and by Frontierland each day. When the park opened, the boat was named for Admiral Joe Fowler, who led the construction of Disneyland and the Magic Kingdom after retiring from the U.S. Navy. This boat was damaged in 1980 during an incident while in drydock backstage, and the vessel was ultimately scrapped. Two years later, the bell from the ship was moved to one of the trains on the Walt Disney World Railroad, the *Roy O. Disney*.

In 1973, a second riverboat was added in honor of Richard F. Irvine, who had multiple connections to the Walt Disney company throughout his life. Personally, he was Walt's eye doctor, but his professional relationship with the company went much further. He had worked as an art director for Disney on films including *The Three Caballeros* and *Victory Through Airpower*, and he worked extensively on the design of Disneyland, the attractions showcased in the 1964 New York World's Fair, and he eventually became CEO of Walt Disney Imagineering.

The *Richard F. Irvine* riverboat still runs in Liberty Square, though under a different name: the *Liberty Belle*. Following the common trend of using the word "liberty" as the primary adjective of the land, Imagineers felt the name would be more memorable with a closer tie to the land the riverboat is housed in. Richard F. Irvine's name has been reused for Disney watercraft since 1999 when one of the ferry boats that transports guests between the Transportation and Ticket Center and the Magic Kingdom was named after him. The other ferry boats have since been named Admiral Joe Fowler and General Joe Potter, who joined the company as vice president of Florida Planning in 1965 following an Army career and time spent working as the governor of the Panama Canal Zone.

Building the Haunted Mansion

For the most part, Liberty Square gives off a very "New England" feel; however, there is one major exception: the Haunted Mansion. The architectural style of the mansion is much more similar to a home you might find in the Hudson River Valley of New York than those from colonial New England towns. In contrast with the rest of the land, the Haunted Mansion's design is based more on eerie fictional tales like "The Legend of Sleepy Hollow," and some of the works by Edgar Allan Poe.

Some elements of the building's design are based on the Harry Packer Mansion. This 1874 Victorian-style mansion is located in Jim Thorpe, Pennsylvania, between a small mountain range in the northeastern part of the state. The mansion was originally built as a wedding gift to Harry Packer from his father, who had become wealthy due to his work on the Lehigh Valley Railroad and Lehigh University. Though Harry died of a kidney ailment at the young age of 34, his wife, Mary, continued to live in the home and raised several adopted children there until her death in 1911. Following Mary's passing, the mansion went through a couple of owners before it was ultimately abandoned due to the large amounts of repairs that would be needed to make the mansion functional. In addition to the lack of working plumbing and electricity, there were growing concerns about the building's structure that would need to be addressed. Finally, in 1983 the mansion was purchased by Patricia and Robert Handwerk, who have repaired the entire mansion, returning it to its original stately elegance. It has since been owned by the family and is run as a bed and breakfast that also holds special events like wine tastings and murder mystery nights.

No murders have ever taken place at the Harry Packer mansion, and despite the themed events hosted there today being a fun source of entertainment, the stories told during the events are based on the lives of the mansion's original owners, but are indeed fictional. Of course, like any good 100+ year old bed and breakfast, it would not be surprising to learn that some guests believe the building to be haunted, though no murders have been confirmed on the property, despite the mansion's official website, MurderMansion.com.

What was it then that caught the attention of Disney Imagineers? The building's architecture alone was enough to inspire much of the external design of the Haunted Mansion in Walt Disney World. Both buildings would fit in well as the setting for a work of gothic literature or a classic horror movie. The brick work, Norman blind-arcading, and vaulted ceilings are just a few of the similarities that the exteriors of both buildings share. Additionally, the Harry Packer mansion is located atop a relatively steep hill. While the Haunted Mansion is not necessarily on a "hill," it is on a higher level of ground.

One reason for this design is simply that of forced perspective, which we see in many places around Disney World, but another is to set the story for the attraction. If guests were able to leave the Hall of Presidents or the *Liberty Belle* only to walk a few feet and find themselves next to a cemetery plot and being invited into some mysterious doorway by a spooky maid or butler, they would likely be confused. Rather than squeezing this grand attraction into the rest of the colonial-era buildings in Liberty Square, setting it back atop a hill some distance away helps stage the story that this attraction is different from the rest of the "town." The way the building looms over guests on their walk over makes it appear larger than it actually is, but it also gives off an unsettling feeling, particularly as guests turn a corner in the queue making the mansion's "front door" come into view while they are still trudging through the cemetery.

If the attraction were to appear welcoming, friendly cast members would happily usher guests right through the front door and into the ride, but this is not the case (for the Haunted

Mansion or for the Harry Packer Mansion, which takes full advantage of the spooky exterior design during promotions for murder mystery nights). Imagineers also wanted to increase the scare factor of the mansion's exterior in comparison to its Disneyland counterpart, which although a bit spooky is much less focused on making guests feel as though the building is hovering over them. The less sinister appearance of Disneyland's mansion initially led some guests to believe that the ride was appropriate for all ages, and while we tend to think of the Haunted Mansion as more playfully spooky than actually scary, it is not difficult to see how it has the ability to frighten children. In an effort to portray the mansion as a scarier attraction, Imagineers designed the exterior of the Disney World mansion to give this impression to guests before they would even enter the queue.

Additional "haunted houses" that Imagineers considered when looking for inspiration to design the Haunted Mansion came from the Winchester Mystery House and the (fictional) home seen in the 1963 film, *The Haunting*. Though *The Haunting* is a British-made film, the story takes place in a traditional New England home that through its haunting becomes alive. You may not realize it initially, but the idea that the home seen in the film is actually "alive" itself helped inspire the storyline and design of the Haunted Mansion. Both the home in the film and the Haunted Mansion feature touches like doors opening and closing, knockers moving on their own, and doors "breathing" in and out. The Haunted Mansion is also meant to appear rather alive, in that guests are entering into a place that is home to 999 "happy haunts," some of which may have become part of the building itself. Next time you visit the Haunted Mansion, take a close and careful look at some of the smaller architectural details, like the moldings in the queue for instance, and you may see what I mean. *The Haunting* may also be part of the inspiration behind one of the best-loved pieces of the Haunted Mansion: the ghoulish wallpaper that has risen to popularity among fans and has become part of everything from luxury handbags to custom MagicBands.

The Winchester Mystery House was the home of Winchester rifle heiress Sarah Winchester. Winchester inherited a large sum of money following the death of her husband who had suffered from tuberculosis. Historians estimate that her husband's will combined with her overseeing the rifle company left her with an income of about $1,000/day, which was an astronomical amount of money to come into during the late 19th century.

Construction of the mansion that would later become known as the Winchester Mystery House began in 1884 when Sarah Winchester purchased a partially built farmhouse in San Jose, California. As the small farmhouse began a transformation into a mansion, the building took on Queen Anne-style Victorian architecture, and it quickly became a seven-story home. As construction would have otherwise come to an end, she ordered the workmen to continue building. She believed that the ghosts of people who had died from Winchester rifles were reaching out to her from the beyond and instructing her to continue construction. Per the ghosts' requests, construction continued until Sarah's death in 1922. The continued construction led to a stately mansion, expertly decorated by Sarah with ornate moldings and antique chandeliers, but it also developed a strange layout. As construction went on, Sarah requested some unusual architectural designs per the request of the lost souls. The finished product is a grand Victorian mansion filled with oddities like staircases that lead to nowhere, doors that open to the outside, and hallways with dead ends. The house today is situated on six acres of land and features a total of 160 rooms. It is a national historic site and is open to the public for tours.

The Winchester Mystery House not only inspired some of the general design elements of the Haunted Mansion, it is also the inspiration for one show scene in particular. The Endless Staircase scene is a reference to the strange construction of the Winchester Mystery House. With staircases leading into the ceiling or other staircases, and ghostly footprints leaving their mark on them, the scene represents Sarah Winchester's belief that the victims of the Winchester rifle were haunting the house she was building. Although the Haunted Mansion's séance room is not inspired by Winchesther house, the latter does contain a séance room where she would routinely try to make contact with the ghosts she felt were there. Another inspiration for the Haunted Mansion's Endless Staircase is the painting *Relativity* by Dutch artist M.C. Escher.

Aside from the mansion itself, what is the first thing guests can expect to see when they enter the attraction? The answer should be a cast member, though perhaps not the typical smiling faces we are used to seeing at Disney World. These maids and butlers to the Ghost Host have every reason to appear spooked and a bit unhappy—the master of the mansion, as guests find out when they enter the Stretching Room, is no longer with us, so the cast members here are in mourning.

Guests may also notice the hearse as they walk down the queue toward the mansion. Disneyland's hearse was purchased by the Disney company for a new show that was in the production stages but was eventually scrapped. Though there are few records regarding the hearse's uses and whereabouts before the company purchased it, we do know that Disney sought it out from an antiques dealer and that it is estimated to be from the mid to late 19th century. When the Disneyland show was cancelled, Imagineer Bob Baranick came up with adding it to the front portion of the queue outside of Haunted Mansion, and Imagineer Tony Baxter suggested the ghost horse detail. Another hearse, also an antique, was later added to the Disney World attraction.

The hearse outside of the Haunted Mansion in Disney World was used as a Hollywood prop before making its way to the Magic Kingdom. The hearse was used to transport Katie Elder's body in the classic 1965 John Wayne film, *The Sons of Katie Elder*. If you happen to watch the film and are wondering when the hearse will come in, keep an eye out at the 5–6 minute mark. The movie opens with the Elder sons attending their mother's funeral, so the hearse makes a very early appearance.

Ghost Writers

The Haunted Mansion is also home to a number of motifs commonly found in American Gothic literature. Most obvious is the sense of foreboding that guests experience when visiting the attraction, which is common in many works in this genre by authors like Edgar Allan Poe, Nathaniel Hawthorne, and Henry James. Elements of the mansion's exterior, like the dead wreath hanging on the front door, give guests a sense of foreboding for what is to come before they even enter the attraction.

The first similarity to Poe's work comes when guests enter the famous Stretching Room. As guests are told to move to the "dead" center of the room, the doorway which they entered through disappears, and the room begins to stretch. As the Ghost Host says, "this chamber has no windows and no doors," quite like what a character experiences in Poe's "The Cask of Amontillado." In Poe's story, one of the characters becomes enclosed in a small crypt, and struggles to push the brick walls apart in an attempt to escape. This kind of entrapment of being closed in a space with no windows and no doors is called immurement, and while it has not been used for some time, it has historically been a form of imprisonment used to torture criminals in various cultures. Guests riding through the Haunted Mansion will be greeted by this concept once more as they exit the graveyard scene and notice a hand trying to dig itself out of a crypt.

The connections to Poe continue during the ride part of the attraction, with the inclusion of a raven in many of the show scenes. The raven, based on Poe's famed 1845 poem, was originally intended to be the narrator, but Imagineers decided to change directions. The decision did not remove the raven, which is named Lucifer, altogether as he is still present throughout the mansion, occasionally cawing as guests ride by in their Doom Buggies.

The raven can also be found in brass form if you look closely at the top of the organ while you glide past the ballroom scene. The type of organ, as inscribed on the instrument, is a Ravenscroft, which is a reference to Thurl Ravenscroft, who in the Haunted Mansion provided the voicework for the lead singing busts in the graveyard scene. An organ with a raven, along with the Ravenscroft inscription, may also be found in the attraction's interactive queue, where guests are able to play the organ themselves and perhaps even hear Thurl's featured song, "Grim Grinning Ghosts."

A more obscure work by Edgar Allan Poe is represented in the mansion when guests pass by a coffin whose occupant is pushing on the lid trying to escape. In addition to this scene serving as a playfully spooky piece of theming, it was inspired by Poe's "The Premature Burial." The story focuses on a character who is buried alive, and thus is desperately trying to push open the lid of the coffin to escape, like the figure in the attraction.

Another connection between Poe's work and the Haunted Mansion comes with the voice of the Ghost Host, Paul Frees. Frees is well-known today for his role as the Ghost Host and as the voice behind animated characters like Ludwig Von Drake and Boris Badenov in *The Adventures of Rocky and Bullwinkle*, but he also worked as a narrator of spooky literature like Edgar Allan Poe's "The Tell Tale Heart."

In the Haunted Mansion's early stages of design, the Imagineers originally intended for it to be a walk-through. In one version, the setting would have been a New England countryside which would draw inspiration from Washington Irving's "The Legend of Sleepy Hollow" (though Irving's story takes place in a Dutch settlement town in New York), with the Headless Horseman as the "star" character.

The horseman may not make an appearance in the attraction, but during Mickey's Not So Scary Halloween Party, he does take a fateful ride through the park, kicking off the Boo to You Parade.

Nautical Lore

A connection to the sea is not one of the immediate elements of the Haunted Mansion that guests notice, but it is worked into the attraction's design. Beginning with the interactive queue, guests entering the attraction will pass the grave for Captain Culpepper Clyne, a character based on Imagineer Ken Anderson's original concept for a sea captain. As the design process for the attraction moved along, the captain idea was scrapped only to be revived much later with the addition of the interactive queue.

The other seaman guests may encounter on the attraction happens while on the ride. Imagineer Marc Davis was also inspired to create sea captain characters, one of which still hangs inside the show building. While some nautical concepts were inspired by the idea of adding a tribute to those lost at sea, and the general sense of fear that can come with a shipwreck,

Davis' captains are the product of his work on Pirates of the Caribbean. None of his designs were duplicated between the two attractions, but when comparing the concept art for the two side by side (particularly with the ideas for the Haunted Mansion that never came to be), it becomes more evident that the same Imagineer had a hand in both attractions.

Early concepts for the Haunted Mansion (by Davis) also understood the entire attraction as one tale of entertaining nautical horror. Where we may be tempted to view the nautical theme as the original "story" of the mansion, Davis believed that the attraction would work better with different parts of the theme just blending into one another without one set storyline. Without a single storyline to go with the nautical theme, the idea was eventually rejected, leaving us with only the glimpses into the ride's nautical past. Guests visiting Disneyland may notice that the mansion's weather vane features a sailing ship, though Disney World's Mansion features a bat instead.

Had the sea captain theme come to be, Imagineers Rolly Crump and Yale Gracey (after whom "Master Gracey" is named) would have continued work on the special effects that would have brought the theme to life. A proposed story for the captain was to have the character return from beyond the grave with the intention of murdering his bride by locking her away, likely behind the brick walls of his fireplace. In a concept that seems to be straight out of any random work of American Gothic literature, the scene would have been accompanied by effects similar to the Pepper's Ghost effect guests see in the ballroom scene today.

Tombstone Tributes

As many Disney fans are well-aware, the names on the tombstones in the queue of the Haunted Mansion refer to the Imagineers who worked on the attraction. Master Gracey's tombstone has fallen victim to the fan theory that Master Gracey is the Ghost Host. While this was not originally the official storyline, as "Gracey" was a reference to Imagineer Yale Gracey who designed many of the attraction's special effects, the theory has stuck so well with the fan community that it is almost an excepted part of Haunted Mansion lore today. The fan theory even inspired the use of the name "Master Gracey" for the owner of the mansion in *The Haunted Mansion* film that debuted in 2003.

Another recognizable tombstone is Madame Leota's, which features the catchy epitaph, "DEAR SWEET LEOTA, BELOVED BY ALL, IN REGIONS BEYOND NOW, BUT HAVING A BALL." Her tombstone was updated in 2002 to allow the sculpture of her face to open and close her eyes, offering an additional spook for guests just before they enter the mansion. Guests know that Madame Leota is a fortune teller once they visit the séance room within the mansion, but they may not realize the official story of how she came to be at there. As the story goes, Madame Leota fled the Salem Witch Trials as a fortune teller, and she moved to the street next to the mansion where she opened her shop, Memento Mori. Even after death she still hasn't left the mansion's neighborhood as she now resides within its walls as one of the 999 happy haunts.

If we want to discuss inaccuracies in American history, at least in the way that stories are created for various areas of the parks, Madame Leota's story is one that does not quite fit. The Haunted Mansion's architecture is sometimes described as "pre-Revolutionary," but other times mentioned as based on the 1874 Harry Packer Estate. While there are certain elements of the architecture that could be reminiscent of a pre-Revolutionary Gothic mansion, the mid to late 19th century seems more plausible. Regardless of when the mansion was built, Madame Leota's story of fleeing the Salem Witch Trials does not add up. The victims of those trials in 1692 were innocent people—not witches or fortune tellers. Furthermore, none of the victims were accused of being fortune tellers. These basic facts make Madame Leota's storyline questionable. And the story becomes even more uncertain when we consider that if the mansion was indeed built in the 19th century, Madame Leota would have been deceased long before she'd be able to haunt the mansion—which gets into a whole different convoluted question of where her soul was during that awkward time between her death and the construction of the mansion. Regardless of the timing of Madame Leota's arrival, death, and the completion of the Mansion, her story loses any realistic basis it may have had in American history when the decision was made to cast her as a fortune teller fleeing Salem.

Other Imagineers featured in tombstones along the mansion's grounds include sculptor Blaine Gibson and Harriet Burns, whose tombstone serves as an honor to her being the "First Lady" of Imagineering. Among the interactive queue, a "writer" tomb was added near the composer and the captain, as well as the Dread family statues. The Dread family appears to be a typical family worked into the Haunted Mansion setting. A closer look reveals that the statues represent a murder mystery that guests can play while they wait in line. To play the game, read the epitaphs beneath each of the statues and use the symbols on the monuments to determine who murdered who.

One more quick note before we leave the mansion—though the grounds where the tombstones are, as well as the last scene of the ride before the hitchhiking ghosts, are often referred to as "graveyards," (by Disney and by fans), this is actually an incorrect usage of the word. A graveyard is located on church grounds, while a cemetery is not. Additionally, some of the art work, particularly the designs of the "death heads" on the tombstones guests may be able to see (given the dark lighting) in the final cemetery scene, would be much more at home in colonial New England than they would in the Hudson River Valley of New York. While death heads were prevalent throughout this time period, varying designs can be traced to different regions. Death heads correspond to the region where the person who carved them is located, as each carver used a slightly different design (and designs changed as religious views changed). It is possible that a cemetery would have death heads from a different region, assuming the family purchasing the tombstone was wealthy enough to commission a stone from a preferred designer farther away, but "farther away" in this instance would not likely mean taking a New England design outside of New England. It is possible, though doubtful, that such tombstones would exist in the approximate location of where we would find the mansion in real life.

CHAPTER THREE

Frontierland

Frontierland takes guests from the birth of the United States in Liberty Square to the next century, where the country is going full speed toward a western expansion. "Westward bound, Dr. Franklin, to new frontiers!" (Oh wait, wrong show. Don't worry, we'll get to Epcot later.)

In all seriousness, guests coming from Liberty Square have one extra hint (aside from the obvious theming) that lets them know they are moving forward in time. The addresses by the doors of the buildings in Liberty Square increase in number as they approach Frontierland. To determine the year of the specific building and where you are in "time," add an 18 to the existing numbers. When you reach Pecos Bill Tall Tale Inn and Café, you'll have reached 1878!

Frontierland, like most areas found in the Magic Kingdom and Disneyland, are based significantly on Walt's passions and sense of nostalgia. Walt was fascinated by the history of western expansion, and had a deep though at times almost mythological understanding of important figures in the time period like Mark Twain, as seen with Tom Sawyer Island. He also, as we know, spent a considerable amount of time in Hollywood, with some of the greatest classic films (including westerns) being created during his lifetime. His own characters would even be animated in western sequences complete with coonskin caps on occasion. And one of Walt's favorite live-action films and historical figures to deal with in the most nostalgic sense was Davy Crockett. With Walt's view of the American West based in fact yet so romanticized, it is easy to understand how the Frontierland areas of the parks turned out the same way.

Where exactly is the Magic Kingdom's Frontierland? Coming from Liberty Square, Frontierland travels west, chronologically. Considering that Liberty Square represents a time that goes at the latest into the late 1700s or early 1800s, the "west" in this period would have only been so far as states like Ohio, Indiana, Michigan, Illinois, Wisconsin, Minnesota, and Iowa. Americans in the early 19th century were not yet thinking of the West the same way we might today. As such, the Rivers of America (though there is nothing really distinctive to make you aware if you did not already know) are meant to allude to the Mississippi and Ohio rivers. Having the river on one side of Frontierland when walking from Liberty Square with the buildings slowly modernizing and becoming more western on the other side of the street is all part of how the Imagineers worked to create a seamless transition between the two lands.

The broad expanse of the American West covered in Frontierland as guests walk closer to Splash Mountain and Big Thunder Mountain Railroad creates a kind of culture clash when we think about the two different kinds of "West" represented here. The "West" we think of when we hear the name Daniel Boone or think of a classic western movie is not the same kind of "West" as turn-of-the-century Ohio. Rather than making any one narrative extremely accurate, the design of Frontierland allows the more positive aspects of both time periods involved in the American West to create a more pleasant environment. (If this part of the park were truly accurate to the 19th century American West, guests would see all kinds of lawless behavior, and general filth.) In the same way that slavery is purposefully omitted from any part of Liberty Square, Frontierland sheds no light on the mistreatment of Native Americans or Chinese immigrants that existed in the 19th century in this part of the country.

Speaking of Chinese immigrants, remember the railroad we discussed earlier? An accurate retelling of the railroad going through Frontierland would have came with some mention of how the railroad was built. During the construction of the Transcontinental Railroad in the 1860s, the industry was fighting labor shortages due to the up-and-coming Nevada Silver Rush. By 1865, an industry leader by the name of Charles

Crocker found a solution to the problem by hiring Chinese immigrants who were flooding into the country and using them as cheap labor (for what was often a difficult and dangerous job).

On top of being severely underpaid for their work, Chinese immigrants during this time faced waves of racism from other Americans, leading up to the Chinese Exclusion Act in 1882. While this dark time in American history may have no place in a family-friendly theme park, it is worth noting that for all of the emphasis that the park places on the railroad and its history, the recollection of the primary group responsible for building said railroad is excluded from the story.

Country Bear Jamboree

This classic Frontierland audio-animatronic show was never intended for the Magic Kingdom at all. When the concept was developed for the Country Bear Jamboree, the original plan was to feature the show at Disney's Mineral King Ski Resort.

In 1965, just about one month after publicly announcing plans to build the Magic Kingdom, Disney seemed to be moving right along with plans for opening a ski resort in the Mineral King region of Sequoia National Forest. While a large-scale entertainment company building a resort within a national park may seem completely outlandish to us today, in 1965 the National Forest Service was fully on board with the idea. The service invited companies to submit proposals for the construction of a ski resort for a valley in Mineral King, and the Disney company was ultimately chosen from among the other five offers.

In a turn of events that seems overly ambitious considering the recent announcement of the new park in Florida, Walt was interested in building the Mineral King Resort because he had visited the area and enjoyed its beauty, and he believed that having a resort in the location would further preserve the area's appeal and allow more people to experience it for themselves. Even though he and his company had never built, owned, or operated a ski resort, prior to 1955 they had not accomplished those things for a theme park either. Like Disneyland, Walt planned on relying on additional entertainment offerings and guest services that far exceeded those offered by competitors in an effort to set the resort apart from the crowd. In the case of Mineral King, he also recognized the need to make the resort a more unique and memorable experience, as a ski resort is not the most profitable venture when based around skiing alone. In terms of entertainment, Walt envisioned a movie theater, figure skating performances, tennis courts, golf courts, upwards of seven or eight restaurants, and a musical audio-animatronic bear show.

Though Walt was entirely serious about the resort, which reportedly had a planned cost of $35 million (to Disneyland's $17 million), activists were not pleased with an entertainment company setting up shop in a national forest. The proposal's opposition noted that the area where the resort would have been built was a game refuge, and as such should not have a commercialized tourist attraction on site.

Following Walt's death in 1966, the Imagineers intended to keep the project alive if for nothing else than for Walt's legacy. They worked on tying up the loose ends within the design phase of the project, which included plans for the construction of a stretch of highway that would bring the guests up to the resort. By 1969, an official announcement was released saying that the resort would be ready and open to the public by the time skiing would begin for the season in 1973.

By this time, the opposition movement against the resort was gaining speed. Residents in the state wore shirts and displayed bumper stickers on their cars exhibiting sayings like "Keep Mineral King Natural." Stewart Udall, who at the time was Secretary of the Interior, expressed concerns about the installation of a highway, suggesting a monorail or some other less invasive form of transportation instead.

By 1972 the resort's planned opening date was still intended to be only one year away, but Imagineers were still going back to the drawing board. This time, they decided to decrease the size of the resort, and they opted to use Walt's original idea of transporting guests to the resort via a cog railway instead of building the planned road. While there were hopes that this decision would appease the naturalists, the true motivation behind the decision was likely more finance related than anything. Imagineers looked at the opening of Disney World one year before, and reflected on how the planned budget was $70 million, but in reality the park had ended up costing the company $400 million.

Though Mineral King was located right next to Sequoia National Park, the area where the resort would have been built was not part of the park, thus placing it in a gray area. To some extent, increased visitation would be a positive outcome of the resort, as more people would be able to come and experience the region's beauty, but it would likely lead to increased industrialization since the area was not protected in the same way as a national park. Despite the opposition, some people including Ronald Reagan (who was governor of California during this time) continued to support the idea.

Eventually, the National Environmental Policy Act was enacted by Congress, which would have required a lengthy study to be taken in the area before any construction plans could move forward. Simultaneously, various groups with disagreements over how to deal with the land in Mineral King ended up making a Supreme Court case out of it. By 1978, the land was officially designated as part of Sequoia National Park, and no more bargaining could be made on any front regarding the possibility of building there. At this point Disney executives began to agree that having the ski resort in any location would not be worth the hassle, and that they would be better off focusing their energy on a different way of remembering Walt's legacy.

In our current society, many of us are more inclined to say that our national parks, and even the national forests bordering them, should be preserved and kept away from commercialization. Though many people did agree with this sentiment in the 1970s, including some Imagineers who were brought along later to work on the project, the unfortunate outcome for the Disney company was the hours of time that had been spent working on a failed project. Most unbuilt Disney concepts are reworked to fit a different time or location, where the initial period spent working on the concept does not seem wasted. The Mineral King project may have served as some of the inspiration for the Wilderness Lodge, though an Imagineer has never said just that. The one real piece of Mineral King design concepts that we can experience today is the Country Bear Jamboree.

Marc Davis, the leading Imagineer for the Country Bear Jamboree (and Pirates of the Caribbean), once recalled showing Walt some of the artwork planned for the attractions in his office. Walt enjoyed seeing the artwork and especially got a big laugh out of seeing some of the bears in the concept pieces, though Davis remembered him looking quite terrible and he attributed his appearance to the recent surgery he had undergone for his lung.

Upon leaving Davis' office that day, Walt started to walk away but then stopped to turn around and say "good-bye." Saying good-bye may seem like a very normal thing to do, but Walt was someone who would very rarely ever say good-bye. He much preferred "see you later," or would mention that they should make plans to see each other again soon, believing that good-bye felt too formal or sad depending on the situation. Soon after saying good-bye to Davis, Walt checked into St. Joseph's Hospital in Los Angeles where he died from complications from lung cancer.

Pirates of the Caribbean is touted as the last attraction that Walt Disney personally worked on before his death. And while Walt may have been more involved with Pirates of the Caribbean, some of the last artwork and concepts he viewed and discussed before his death were actually of both Pirates of the Caribbean and the Country Bear Jamboree.

After Walt's death, plans continued for the Country Bear Jamboree, and when the Magic Kingdom opened the show was one of only three attractions that were unique to that park and not a duplicate of an attraction in Disneyland. (The Hall of Presidents and the Mickey Mouse Revue were the other two.) The success of the Country Bear Jamboree in Florida led to the show being added to Disneyland, where eventually an entire land was named "Bear Country" as a result. The Disneyland show opening also marks the first time an attraction at Disney World was replicated for Disneyland. Prior to 2002, different versions of the original show with either a family vacation or a Christmas theme were sometimes performed, but unfortunately these versions have not existed in years and it is doubtful that they will ever make a comeback.

Recognize any of the voices in the Country Bear Jamboree? Sometimes it can be difficult to pick up on, but you can actually find some of the same voice actors in attractions all over Disney World. In the Country Bear Jamboree, for instance, Loulie Jean Norman, who voices Bubbles (the slightly higher pitched of the three bears who sing "All the Guys That Turn Me On Turn Me Down"), can also be found in the Haunted Mansion. Next time you ride through the graveyard scene, before entering the room with the hitchhiking ghosts, keep an eye and ear out for Loulie as the opera-singing ghost on your right. Still wondering where you've heard her voice before? That would be the theme song for the original Star Trek television series.

The other two triplets in this sequence are voiced by Jackie Ward, primarily known for her 1963 one-hit-wonder *Wonderful Summer*, and Peggy Clark, most known for her role as Miss Carter in the 1949 film *No Way Back*.

Melvin the moose, who is hanging on the wall to the right of the stage, is voiced by Bill Lee, most known for his voicework as Roger in *101 Dalmations* and very briefly in the beginning of *Cinderella* as the title character's father.

Next to Melvin you'll find Buff, voiced by Thurl Ravenscroft, one of the many voices featured in Pirates of the Caribbean, the Haunted Mansion, and Walt Disney's Enchanted Tiki Room. As for voicework outside of Disney, Thurl is also the voice behind Frosted Flakes' Tony the Tiger.

The most famous, or at least popular among fans of the show, is the voice of Big Al. The character's name is a nod to Al Bertino, who worked on creating the show with Marc Davis. Whether it be for the comedic reliefs his character provides or that all too catchy-yet-sobering ditty, *Blood on the Saddle*, Big Al steals the show every time. Big Al's voice is none other than Tex Ritter, classic American country singer and father of John Ritter. Nicknamed "America's Most Beloved Cowboy," his voice seems to have found the perfect home within the walls of Pioneer Hall at the Country Bear Jamboree. Ritter was inducted into the Country Music Hall of Fame in 1964, and is also known for helping to start the United Cerebral Palsy organization after learning that his son Thomas had the condition. Ritter died only a couple of years after the Magic Kingdom opened, but his voice can still be heard each day in the park thanks to Big Al and the rest of the Country Bears.

Old McDonald

For a bit of pop-culture history tucked away in Frontierland, visit the Golden Oak Outpost, located right across from Pecos Bill Tall Tale Inn & Café on the pathway that leads to Adventureland. Currently a seasonally open snack spot, this kiosk was the McDonalds Fry Cart that operated in Frontierland from 1999 to 2007.

Like everything else in Disney, even a McDonalds Fry Cart would come with a backstory fitting the theme of the land. In a pun-filled storyline, Old McDonald set up his fry cart to cash in on all of the prospectors who were heading west in search of gold, lending to the tagline that was plastered on the front of the cart, "There's gold in them thar fries!" McDonald opened his cart in 1853, which makes sense chronologically with the Gold Rush beginning in 1849. As the story goes, a flood in 1855 took the cart and damaged it, but McDonald repaired it and added the wood planks where guests would order their fries so as to avoid getting their boots muddy.

This addition to the story is actually in reference to specific years within the relationship between McDonalds and the Disney company. The oldest continually operating McDonalds restaurant was opened in 1953, which led Disney Imagineers to include "53" on the signage for the fry cart. That same year, McDonalds executive Ray Croc had suggested to the McDonald brothers (Dick and Mac) that they should expand their business into a franchise. One year later, Kroc wrote to Walt Disney inquiring if there would be any interest in placing a McDonalds franchise in Disneyland when it opened. Walt declined to answer personally, sending the letter to concessions management who apparently never got back to Kroc. In 1955, the same year that Disneyland opened, Kroc opened the first franchised McDonalds location.

Since the fry cart closed in 2007, the kiosk has been renamed the Golden Oak Outpost, and is open seasonally based on crowd projections in the park. It currently uses a rotating menu, offering items like chicken nuggets and specialty waffle fries. The name Golden Oak is a nod to a small piece of Disney history, as it refers to the Golden Oak Ranch in California where many live-action movies and television scenes were filmed, including some segments of *The Mickey Mouse Club*. The luxury private residential community Golden Oak, located just outside of Walt Disney World, is similarly named.

Nice and Juicy!

Another bit of pop-culture history was made in Frontierland in the 1980s: the turkey leg. While this mammoth "snack" is sold at a variety of locations across Disney parks today, its original location was the cart in Frontierland, near the Country Bear Jamboree, where it is still being sold today. The turkey leg itself was a classic piece of Americana sold at various fairs and carnivals across the country before Disney ever began selling them in the Magic Kingdom.

Falsely rumored to be emu meat rather than turkey meat, one leg weighs in at just over 1,000 calories. Disney apparently intended for guests to share them, and this method of eating them combined with how many calories guests should be walking off in the parks each day in theory at least should make consuming a turkey leg not as bad as it sounds.

Turkey legs have proved to be so popular among Disney guests they have become something of a pop-culture novelty. Merchandise now exists designed exclusively around the turkey leg branding. Everything from t-shirts, to keychains and even magnets that resemble the smoky legs are sold throughout Disney World.

Another tidbit of turkey history at Disney World is that Thanksgiving turkeys pardoned by U.S. presidents have been known to make their way to the resort (or to Disneyland). The practice began following a ceremony in the White House Rose Garden where George W. Bush pardoned two birds that were later sent to Disney World. As the years went on, the Disney company decided that the upkeep and care for pardoned turkeys were more time consuming than the pardoning was worth, and the turkeys began being sent to George Washington's Mount Vernon estate instead. (Today the turkeys are sent to a farm in Morven Park, Virginia.)

Tom Sawyer Island

A walkthrough representation of one of the most famous works of American literature also exists in Frontierland. Without a doubt one of the most under-visited attractions in the Magic Kingdom is Tom Sawyer Island. As Mark Twain's novel is still on the agenda for many schoolchildren, the lack of interest in visiting the island among guests is likely due to it being a walkthrough attraction. In recent years, walking attractions (or standing ones in the case of the CircleVision films offered at Epcot) have dwindled in popularity. Whether it be that guests do not want to stand on their tired feet when they have the opportunity to partake in a seated attraction instead, or guests no longer have the attention spans to explore on their own, Tom Sawyer Island is extremely under-visited.

As for its accuracy to the famed American novel? The island allows guest to walk through various scenes from the book without ever running into any of the characters, so it's about as accurate as any walkthrough attraction can be. Any issues that modern society outside of the Magic Kingdom may run into when reading some of the racial slurs that are present in the written work do not exist on the island simply because it portrays the book's setting and nothing else. Guests may explore the forts and caves, and the famous whitewashed fence, without the characters present. A notable inclusion is Fort Langhorn, a reference to Samuel Langhorn Clemens (Mark Twain), and is said to be designed using inspiration from a childhood fort that Walt and Roy built while growing up.

Big Thunder Mountain Railroad

Big Thunder Mountain Railroad is Frontierland's runaway mine train roller-coaster through a setting based on Monument Valley in Utah. In a change from the usual flatter landscapes of Florida, Thunder Mountain is surrounded by rockwork and plateaus that give the area a more authentic western feel. When the attraction opened in 1980, the total cost of the project rose to $17 million, more than the total cost of Disneyland when the park opened in 1955. A reported $300,000 was spent on the authentic props seen throughout the attraction, including the wooden mine flume and ore-hauling wagon.

The size of Big Thunder Mountain Railroad has often been overlooked in recent years, especially now that Expedition Everest exists, but there are some interesting statistics regarding the size and scope of the attraction. The peak of the mountain reaches 197 feet tall, the total land area taken up by the attraction is about two acres, and the construction used 650 tons of steel, 4,675 tons of Disney-created "mud," and about 9,000 gallons of paint. In recent years, Big Thunder Mountain Railroad became one of the first attractions to feature an interactive queue, with components designed to make a wait time more enjoyable while providing additional backstory information for the attraction.

The story of Big Thunder Mountain Railroad, if you can't tell by the queue, focuses on the Gold Rush. As the story goes, the miners looking to prospect at the mountain had arrived in the town of Tumbleweed (hence the small references to Tumbleweed you may find throughout the queue). Unbeknownst to them, the mountain was part of an Apache burial ground, referred to by the local tribe as Big Thunder. The name refers to the general calamity that ensues when prospectors attempt to take a train through the area, which causes problems like cave-ins, floods, and an all-around crazy ride. The problems continued for some time, until the miners ultimately gave up on Big Thunder and left to prospect elsewhere.

Years later, a wealthy business owner by the name of Barnabas Bullion became interested in pursuing a mining operation at the mountain, and the old railroad was opened back up. In addition to returning the mine to its original operation, the new owner created a kind of tourist attraction allowing visitors to get a feel for mining aboard one of the trains, which is where guests come into play. Today guests can see a portrait of Barnabas in the attraction's queue, though the person depicted is Imagineer Tony Baxter.

This story is all well and good, and knowing the story while wandering through the queue will allow you to get more out of the attraction, as many of the smaller details make more sense given the ride's plot. However, the small mention of Native

Americans naming the mountain does little justice for their culture, and the idea that the settlers were prospecting on a native burial ground is obviously not something most businesses would want to be a part of today. Then, of course, there is the continued trend of leaving out the group of people who were responsible for building many of these kinds of railroads in the first place—Chinese immigrants.

A final detail of note at Thunder Mountain is the choice of music. The area features instrumentals of American folk classics native to the region or the time period, if not both. One such song was produced in 1844 and is called "Buffalo Gals," though audience members would routinely change the song to refer to their current location, in this case "Tumbleweed Gals." "Hand Me Down My Walking Cane," which was produced during the 1880s, is another famous instrumental (at least in this version) heard while waiting for the ride, as are more modern remakes of older folk music that guests may recognize from the 1950s *Davy Crockett* TV series.

Splash Mountain

Splash Mountain, as many devout Disney fans know, but the majority of guests in the Magic Kingdom probably do not know, is based on the 1946 partially animated, partially live-action film *Song of the South*. We'll cover the film briefly here, because there really is so much to say about it that it would require a separate book. (And thankfully a separate book on the subject exists! If you are interested in *South of the South* I recommend Jim Korkis' book, *Who's Afraid of Song of the South?*) *Song of the South* has become known as the ultimate "banned" Disney film, which fans like to point out in a sense of irony as one of the most popular rides in the Magic Kingdom is based on the work. The film was pulled from theaters in 1986, and never made available on home-video (VHS) in the United States, despite critical acclaim and having won an Oscar for the classic song played every single day in the Magic Kingdom, "Zip-a-Dee-Doo-Dah."

The film is based on the classic Uncle Remus stories which have been a part of American folklore since they were published in 1881 by Joel Chandler Harris. The problem with the film is the treatment of blacks, who many viewers felt were stereotyped into negatively depicted characters for the purpose of entertainment, thus making a joke out of the hardships that freedmen like Uncle Remus would have continued to deal with following the end of slavery.

Some viewers also end up feeling that the film in a way glamorizes slavery, or at least that it glosses over how much of an issue slavery actually was. In most cases, viewers who felt this way do not realize the film takes place after slavery was abolished, as there is no tell-tale sign of a specific year in the film, and the producers were under the assumption that viewers would know the Uncle Remus stories took place later. Of course, the film makes little effort to make the time period entirely clear to a general audience, and even considering the film as a post-Civil War work, it is doubtful that black Americans during the years that followed the war would have happily went along their day-to-day lives as the film seems to depict. (Our knowledge of later history tells us that the end of slavery was unfortunately not always the end of the mistreatment of then-freed slaves, so while the film does take place later it may be somewhat sugar-coated in that sense.)

Other stereotypes in the film include the dialects used by the black actors, and some of their mannerisms in the way they behave with other characters that audiences may take as a jab at their intelligence. And not surprisingly the tar-baby scene where Br'er Fox uses a doll made out of tar to help capture Br'er Rabbit has not sat particularly well with audiences.

The related attraction, Splash Mountain, grew out of the Imagineers' desire to create a classic log-flume ride, and also from the recycled characters of a closed Disneyland show. Imagineer Tony Baxter is credited with coming up with the original idea in an attempt to send more guests to Disneyland's Bear Country, which at the time was only home to the Country Bear Jamboree and a single gift shop. The closing of the America Sings attraction in Disneyland, an audio-animatronic show that delved into the history of American music, also had a hand in the creation of Splash Mountain. When the attraction closed in 1988, many of the audio-animatronic animals were saved and later recast in Splash Mountain (in Disneyland), which opened the following year. The huge success of the attraction on the West Coast led to the construction of its Florida counterpart, with the Magic Kingdom's Splash Mountain opening in 1992.

Tony Baxter has been credited with making the decision to use the film as a basis for the ride as he was trying to put together an attraction that would be able to fit with the theme of Bear Country, include a log flume (that would come to have a 50-foot plunge), and re-use the America Sings characters. The other inspiration for using *Song of the South* seems to be in large part due to the music from the film. The popular songs, particularly "Zip-a-Dee-Doo-Dah," were known to resonate with guests whether or not they were familiar with the film they came from.

There are two noticeable differences between the film and the attraction that are worth noting. The most obvious is the exclusion of Uncle Remus from the ride, and the other is the exclusion of the tar-baby. (The scene with the tar-baby technically exists, but Imagineers used a bees' nest in place of the tar-baby.) Unfortunately, Uncle Remus, or rather the actor who played him and won an Oscar for doing so, James Baskett, was excluded from attending the premiere of the film in 1946. Due to segregation, he was unable to secure a hotel room near the theater where the film was playing, and as a result missed his opportunity to see the premiere. His exclusion from the ride is more than likely the company treading lightly with his character due to the film's opposition. If there were viewers who saw his character in the film as a black stereotype, creating an audio-animatronic of the character would not help the company's public image.

If you want to view the film today, you will have a tough time tracking it down. Occasionally, eBay, yard sales, or flea markets can be the spots where you'd run into a copy of the film, but this has been getting more and more unlikely as time passes and the film is not re-released. Clips of it are available on YouTube, and while you may come across other copies online I would caution against downloading a bootleg version. To learn more about the controversies surrounding the film, picking up Jim Korkis' book will be your best option. Korkis presents the information in the book from an unbiased standpoint, allowing the reader to not only be informed about the controversy, but also to have the ability to come to their own conclusion on the matter.

Western River Expedition

Originally planned for the area currently occupied by Frontierland's mountain range, the Western River Expedition concept would have likely become the most historically-accurate attraction in Frontierland. The entire area, had the concepts developed further, would have been known as Thunder Mesa Mountain, and would have included a re-created Native American village, a canoe-styled flume ride, walking trails, and a runaway mine-train ride similar to what became Big Thunder Mountain Railroad. The ideas for this area were originally conceived by Marc Davis, who was working off the unused concepts for an indoor Disney theme park in St. Louis, Missouri. This park, had it been built, would have included a Lewis and Clark River Expedition, an exciting adventure based on the pair's actual journey that would take guests along for the ride.

The concept would have made use of an astonishing 100 audio-animatronics, and it would have covered every element of the West, including stagecoach robberies, Native Americans, buffalo, saloon dancers, and cowboys. While the work on the attraction did not get too far, buffalo and prairie dog figures were created for it that have since been moved to the farm scene in Epcot's Living with the Land ride.

There are a couple of reasons why the attraction never came to fruition, but the most problematic was the cost. As you'd imagine, an attraction using 100 audio-animatronics figures would not come cheap. In considering how expensive it was to create Big Thunder Mountain Railroad, it is understandable that an attraction of this scope would have been extremely costly. Another reason was that guests were more interested in the Pirates of the Caribbean attraction than they were in a new concept altogether. Some believe that it is for the best that the attraction never came to be, because despite the premise being based on Lewis and Clark's historic expedition, one of the Native American scenes would have included a rain dance that guests would likely come to see as stereotypical in later years.

Pecos Bill Tall Tale Inn and Café

Pecos Bill is an American folk legend about the roughest and toughest cowboy in the Wild West. The tales of Pecos Bill were likely passed down by word of mouth before ever having been recorded, but we do know that the first published account of a Pecos Bill story was in 1916, in a publication called *The Century Magazine*. The character continued to pop up in short stories and cartoon strips for the next 30 or so years, leading to Pecos Bill's inclusion in a Disney production in 1948. *Melody Time* was released in theaters that year, and the film ends with a finale sequence narrated by Roy Rogers that showcases the adventures of Pecos Bill. Though brief in the grand scheme of a memorable Disney animated sequence, Pecos Bill's character began to grow in popularity, and by the time Imagineering was hard at work designing Frontierland, it only made sense that one of the most famous cowboys be included there.

Within Frontierland, Pecos Bill Tall Tale Inn and Café opened in 1878, as it states on the outside of the building. The restaurant draws on the traditional folklore that Pecos Bill was a more skilled cowboy than anyone else in the West. The most popular tale featuring Peocs Bill was that during a drought in Texas, he dug out the canals that became the Rio Grande, thus saving everyone in need of water. Another popular fable is that while fooling around with his gun one day he shot down all of the stars in the sky above him except for one, thus naming Texas the "Lone Star State." (These legends are listed on a wall inside the restaurant, though with the hectic atmosphere inside, especially during the lunch and dinner rushes, you may not have had a chance to read them.) The story of the café is much simpler than his other tales. In 1878 he decided to open a "watering hole," and after finding customers in his other legendary friends, the restaurant began to keep some of the supplies and other things people left behind (hence the artifacts and decorations you see around the restaurant).

John Texas Slaughter and the King of Pop

Michael Jackson's connection to Walt Disney World is not limited to the former Captain EO attraction in Epcot. In an interview, the pop star admitted that a scene in his music video for the song "Thriller" was inspired by none other than the Frontierland Shootin' Arcade in the Magic Kingdom. Jackson recalled that he saw the skeleton hand reaching out from a grave in the attraction, and felt compelled to use a similar shot in his video.

Another pop-culture reference tucked away by the Frontierland Shootin' Arcade is a poster to the attraction's left that reads, "Texas John Slaughter's Academy of Etiquette will make 'em do what they oughta!" *Texas John Slaughter* was a 1950s TV series, and the rest of the sayings on the poster are part of the show's theme song.

CHAPTER FOUR

Adventureland

"Think Orange Thoughts"

One of Adventureland's greatest ties to the American past is ironically found in a character that has had an off-and-on relationship with the park. The Orange Bird has been part of the Adventureland landscape since the Magic Kingdom opened, initially making appearances outside the Sunshine Pavilion (currently Walt Disney's Enchanted Tiki Room). The character's connection to the Disney company, however, began long before 1971.

Unlike the majority of characters guests see in the parks, the Orange Bird was never produced as part of a Disney film. Instead, he is the result of a corporate sponsorship between the Disney company and the Florida Citrus Commission, a business relationship that has existed since 1941. The partnership initially began so that Donald Duck could be used in the marketing of orange juice in the 1940s. Although you probably haven't seen Donald anywhere near orange juice advertisements lately, this partnership does still exist and is actually one of the longest continually running partnerships between two companies in the United States.

During the Magic Kingdom's construction in 1969, the Florida Citrus Commission became the official sponsor of the Sunshine Pavilion. A contract was drawn up and signed by the two parties on October 22, 1969, declaring the commission an official sponsor of the $3 million then unnamed "bird show." Since there would be such a large presence in the Magic Kingdom for the citrus group, Disney decided to create an official mascot of sorts for the area, and other advertising campaigns that both companies would eventually put out. Disney artist C. Robert "Bob" Moore completed the designs for the character just in time for him to be used in promotional materials for the opening of the park. The Orange Bird quickly became not only a vital piece of promo in advertising Adventureland before the park opened, but an invaluable source of campaign material for orange juice. In both respects, the Orange Bird was featured on Florida billboards, newspapers, magazines, and elsewhere prior to the opening of the Magic Kingdom.

The Orange Bird proved to be popular among guests, primarily those from Florida who had more of a connection to him through his other ad campaigns. Orange Bird's popularity continued to grow throughout the 1970s due to his feature in a self-titled promotional record that was sometimes given out to guests visiting the park. The record was written by the Sherman Brothers with songs performed by former Miss Oklahoma Anita Bryant. Bryant continued to be a part of the marketing campaigns for the Orange Bird for the next couple of years, appearing with the character in both television and print ads.

Unfortunately, the 1970s reign of the Orange Bird ended in a controversial way. Bryant became active in circles that created opposition toward anti-discrimination acts in her hometown of Miami. She also vocalized her stance against homosexuality, which caused boycotts of Florida Citrus products due to her relationship with the company. Bryant's public opinions on homosexuality were stirred by a piece of legislation in Miami that worked to protect the LGBT community from discrimination within the workplace or while finding housing, and the boycotts that followed became the first of their kind to receive such expansive media coverage.

As a result of her controversial statements, the Florida Citrus Commission ended their partnership with Bryant, and the Orange Bird was slowly phased out. While Bryant was not a necessary tie to the Orange Bird, the latest ad campaigns gave her the speaking role to the character who formerly only communicated through orange thought bubbles. With the abrupt removal of Bryant from the campaigns, Orange Bird was left without being able to express himself as he previously had when the two worked together. He was featured in a couple of educational shorts regarding food and nutrition, titled *Foods and Fun: A Nutrition Adventure*, and *The Orange Bird and the Nutrition Bandwagon*, although he waned in popularity as a solo act, and perhaps as a side effect of the drama surrounding Bryant.

Despite the controversies surrounding Bryant, the Florida Citrus Commission renewed their contracts as sponsors of the area in Adventureland until 1986, resulting in the complete removal of all things Orange Bird by the early 1990s. Fans did not see or hear anything about the Orange Bird for quite some time, until he was spotted in Tokyo in 2004. Disney tends to have a strange way of testing out obscure characters in Tokyo Disneyland before deciding whether or not they should be present in Disneyland or Disney World. Oddly enough, with the majority of guests in Tokyo having little or no connection to the character, the Orange Bird was an instant hit, prompting his return to Disney World, at least in the form of limited edition merchandise in 2009. By 2012, guests again were able to spot him in his rightful spot in Adventureland, and today Orange Bird merchandise is sold throughout Disney World.

CHAPTER FIVE

Tomorrowland

Tomorrowland may not be the most "American" location at Walt Disney World, but a closer look reveals some subtle connections to the historical events during the time that this area was being designed. Guests today feel like there is nothing at all futuristic about Tomorrowland, and that's because there really isn't. Tomorrowland looks like the 1960s. It looks like scenes from a 1960s science fiction film were dropped into the middle of Florida. Tomorrowland feels like the moon landing hasn't happened yet.

As much as we envision Walt Disney and his obsession for creating a fantasyland, with his vision of Disneyland as a place where parents and children could have fun together, we have to remember that he was also a realist. He, along with many of the Imagineers involved with designing the parks, were interested in science, particularly in terms of space travel, which during the early 1960s was working toward the goal of a landing on the moon. While Walt did not live to learn of the moon landing in 1969, the design of Tomorrowland shows how inspired he was by the race to get there.

Part of Walt's vision for the future included making sure that the earth would be well taken care of for future generations to enjoy. In designing Epcot (as a planned city, not the theme park), he took great pride in designing the most energy efficient and cleanest forms of transportation to get citizens around the community without emitting fumes into the air. One way he planned to make this possible was using the PeopleMover.

Tomorrowland Transit Authority PeopleMover

The PeopleMover is much more than the little tram that gives guests an overview of Tomorrowland. It is a functioning piece of history for a concept that was part of the Epcot that never came to be. Walt's Epcot would have had numerous forms of clean transportation (another being the monorail), and the PeopleMover would have served as a way for residents to go between their homes in the suburbs to the community center without using a car, or public transportation that would have the same effect on the environment.

The vehicles that make up the PeopleMover would be fuel efficient, and run by a friction-drive system, and as we see in the parks the cars would be able to run on tracks above walkways. The latter point is important in terms of their design for two reasons. One is that riding above the walkway (at least in an open air, otherwise enjoyable ride like the PeopleMover) would be enticing for residents to want to use it, and using the elevated track would also save space on the walkways for other structures, or just open space.

While aboard the PeopleMover, guests are able to view a model of Walt Disney's Progress City, which served as the inspiration for Epcot. What you may not realize from the ride vehicle is that the model of Progress City shown behind the glass is actually only a portion of the complete model. If you happen to come across the footage of Walt Disney describing the original concept for Epcot, you'll notice that the full-size model was much larger. (The footage may be found with a quick search online in clips, and in its entirety on a limited-release DVD.)

Carousel of Progress

Walt Disney's classic audio-animatronic show debuted at the 1964 New York World's Fair, where the concept of a circular theater that rotated around different sets on a stage proved to be a huge success with audiences. When the Fair closed the Carousel of Progress show was moved to Disneyland, where it continued to wow audiences until its closure in 1973. Two years later the Carousel of Progress opened in Disney World, where it is still "performed" today.

As the show is continually performed throughout the day at Disney World, it has the designation as one of the longest continually performing stage shows in American theater. The show encompasses many of the ideas that Walt was passionate about, while including audio-animatronics and show sets that were advanced for their time, and music by renowned songwriting brothers, Richard and Robert Sherman. The show's technological advancements do not stop with the audio-animatronic figures; the concept of the "carousel theater" was also a new and innovative part of the attraction. Imagineers Bob Gurr and Roger E. Broggie were responsible for coming up with the concept for the rotating theater, with the goal of moving the audience around each scene while they remained seated, rather than having to move guests along as they walk to different sets.

The show also blends together two of Walt's most-loved interests—nostalgia and the future. Following an American family as they go through all the new forms of "progress" from the turn of the century to the "present" (or recent past), the show also offers a sense of nostalgia for audience members who may remember certain experiences from their own lives, or have learned about them in stories told by grandparents. These interests are further exemplified in the Sherman brothers' catchy theme song:

> There's a great, big, beautiful tomorrow
> Shining at the end of every day
> There's a great, big, beautiful tomorrow
> And tomorrow's just a dream away
> Man has a dream and that's the start
> He follows his dream with mind and heart
> And when it becomes a reality
> It's a dream come true for you and me
> So there's a great, big, beautiful tomorrow
> Shining at the end of every day
> There's a great, big, beautiful tomorrow
> Just a dream away

General Electric was the original sponsor of the Carousel of Progress, and this point is driven home with the number of appliances shown in the attraction that were manufactured by G.E., though they may be difficult to spot today as the G.E. logo was removed from each item when the sponsorship ended. During the company's 10-year sponsorship, G.E. used the Carousel of Progress as an opportunity to market their products to the millions of guests who would at some point see the show.

The sponsorship started to deteriorate when the attraction opened in Disney World due to newly promoted executives at G.E. who began to feel that the attraction's theme song, "There's a Great Big Beautiful Tomorrow," seemed to imply that guests should hold off on buying new G.E. appliances at present as new and better items would be available "tomorrow." The Sherman Brothers were then tasked with writing a new song to keep the attraction's sponsor happy. The additional song was called "The Best Time of Your Life." and as the title suggests the song was intended to convey the message that now is the time to purchase G.E. appliances.

The show has undergone a number of changes over the years, between the song change to appease G.E., various voice actors taking on the roles of the audio-animatronics, and updates to the final scene through the 1990s. The original voice actor for the role of John, the family's father, was Rex Allen. He was later replaced as John's voice by Andrew Duggan, following his work for other companies like his role in *Charlotte's Web*, while simultaneously (at least in the eyes of Disney executives) making little effort to work with the company. In the latest refurbishment of the attraction, the father's voice is done by *A Christmas Story*'s Jean Shepherd, and Rex was brought back as the voice of the family's grandfather. "There's a Great Big Beautiful Tomorrow" also returned to the show in its latest version, along with the additional wording in the attraction's title, "Walt Disney's Carousel of Progress," with emphasis on Walt's infatuation with the themes the attraction depicts.

Guests today tend to question why the Carousel of Progress exists in Tomorrowland when at present no scene of the attraction is futuristic. If a guest does not agree with this confusion, chances are he or she is skipping the attraction in favor of a more popular ride, or using the show as an air-conditioned naptime. It is unfortunate that one of Walt's most passionate creations is leaving guests confused. In an effort to clear the air, Disney historians like Jim Korkis have mentioned possibilities for how the show can still be relevant to Tomorrowland, namely, that the show is meant to be a historical representation of life on Earth for Tomorrowland's citizens of the future to view between their travels. This story may not have been the intended theme of the Carousel of Progress, but it makes a lot more sense than assuming the "future" or even the "present" is the 1990s.

A little-known tribute in the attraction is a billboard bearing the name "Herb Ryman." Ryman was an Imagineer who was responsible for creating much of the concept art for future attractions. Don't forget to bring your glasses if you want to catch his tribute while watching the show, as you'll need to peer out the family's window in the back of the 1920s scene to read the billboard. The final scene of the attraction also features a tribute to an Imagineer, Marty Sklar, the former vice chairman and principal creative executive for Walt Disney Imagineering. A note on the bulletin board in this scene reads, "Marty called—wants changes," which is not only a reference to Sklar himself, but also to his position where changes for attractions would often be proposed by him as the head of creative.

An even more obscure reference in the attraction is Little Egypt and her connection to the 1893 Chicago World's Fair. Little Egypt is the dancer that the son in the show references as "doing the hoochie coochie" when looking through his father's stereoscope. She was a real-life dancer from the late 19th century named Fatima Djemille, who performed at the 1893 Chicago World's Fair.

Disney's Space Race

Opening in 1975, Space Mountain's ride system was designed by Arrow Development, which was also responsible for Disneyland's Matterhorn roller-coaster that uses a similar system under an obviously different theme. When Disneyland opened, it was unclear among Walt and the Imagineers whether or not thrill rides would do well in the park. The reasoning behind Disneyland after all was the need for a place where parents and children could have fun together, and presumably many children would not be interested in or even able to ride thrill rides. The Matterhorn's popularity prompted work to begin on creating a similar (yet perhaps more thrilling due to the ride taking place in the dark) ride for guests in Disney World.

Space Mountain represents the American interest in space travel and the space race that had recently culminated with the moon landing in 1969. In celebration of space travel, astronauts including Scott Carpenter (Mercury 7), Gordon Cooper (Mercury 9 and Gemini 5), and Jim Irwin (Apollo 15) were all invited to attend the opening celebrations for the ride.

Space Mountain's relation to American history is limited to its vague 1960s–70s style of "futuristic" design, prevalent in the minds of an American people who were arguably more interested in space travel than we are today. This simple theming may be the only hint of American history here, but there are some interesting and little-known tributes in the ride that are noteworthy regardless:

In the queue of Space Mountain, you may have noticed constellation maps with references to far-off galaxies. One such mention is "Disney's Hyperion Resort," a subtle nod to the Walt Disney Studios' former location on Hyperion Avenue in Hollywood.

Like the Carousel of Progress, if your vision allows for it you may catch a tribute to an Imagineer while riding Space Mountain. During the lift hill, look up to the space station above your rocket and see if you can make out "H-NCH." These letters are a reference to Imagineer John Hench, who created the first concept art for the attraction during the 1960s. The reference to "75" under his name, as well as in the attraction's logo, refer to the year that Space Mountain opened. Also in the lift hill, riders come across astronauts that were once featured in an older version of the descent at Spaceship Earth in Epcot.

The robotic dog in the post-show of Space Mountain was originally a nod to RCA, which sponsored the ride from 1975 to 1993. The dog is a futuristic interpretation of Kipper, RCA's icon, and while the sponsorship has been over for a number of years, Kipper still has a home beside the moving walkway guests use to exit the attraction. The post-show includes a couple of references to an extinct Disney attraction as well. The luggage guests walk past during the post-show feature a sticker labeled "Mesa Verde," a reference to the fictional location included in Epcot's former Horizons attraction. A tribute to the former 20,000 Leagues Under the Sea attraction is displayed in the post show, too, on the screen reading "20,000 Lightyears Under the Sea."

Guests may also notice a screen listing "closed sectors," which are abbreviations for rides in the Magic Kingdom that have closed, and "open sectors," for rides that have opened in the recent past. In the same area, a series of "traffic codes" are listed that reference central Florida roads and highways.

CHAPTER SIX

Fantasyland

Fantasyland is based in the culture of European fairy tales, but there are a few parts of Fantasyland that are distinctly American: the antique beauty of Prince Charming Regal Carrousel which harkens back to an earlier time at an American amusement park, the odd protests and press coverage that followed rumors that Mr. Toad's Wild Ride would close, and a turn of events that shows freedom of speech at work. Also under the "American" umbrella, though not in context, just in design, is "it's a small world," which was designed by Mary Blair, and debuted at the 1964 New York World's Fair.

Prince Charming Regal Carrousel

The carrousel guests experience while visiting Fantasyland is not original to any Disney park. It was constructed in 1917 and its original park was the Detroit Palace Garden Park, in Detroit, Michigan. The carrousel, like many amusement attractions during this time period, was built by the Philadelphia Toboggan Company, which had named the attraction Miss Liberty and used a red, white, and blue color scheme. When the Detroit Palace Garden Park went bankrupt, the carrousel was moved to Philadelphia in 1928, where it underwent a refurbishment that involved changing the paint and the name, before it was relocated to Olympic Park in Maplewood, New Jersey.

Olympic Park was open from 1887 to 1965, and during its height it was one of the most popular amusement parks on the East Coast. In addition to traditional rides like the carrousel, the park also featured the largest public swimming pool in the area, live music, dance halls, horse racing, and gardens.

The park's closure which resulted in Disney purchasing the carrousel unfortunately had a long time coming. In 1912, the park had suffered a fire that burned the opera house and dance hall to the ground. The next summer's terrible weather severely impacted the projected attendance, and the owners began to fall into debt. When the ownership ultimately changed to one of the park's largest creditors, failure again ensued as the result of a country fair with poor weather and poor turnout. The next manager for the park had put $50,000 worth of improvements into it, but was found to have committed suicide only after about a month of operating the business. When Prohibition began, the next new owners turned the establishment into a dry park, and focused their efforts on changing the rebuilt opera house into a fun house, and lowering the price of admission in hopes of attracting more guests. The park's owners during the mid-1920s had finally found success, focusing on family-friendly elements like creating an ice cream palace, keeping up with the fun house, and completing the construction of the swimming pool.

At this point, the park had been able to purchase the carrousel, which following its extensive refurbishment featured an imported organ from Italy, decorated with a cymbal, brass drum, snare drum, and dancing figures. It was also shortly after the park purchased the carrousel that the Great Depression hit, delivering a severe blow to attendance. The park's financial woes continued through World War II as the owners struggled to maintain the park's upkeep with limited ability to purchase certain food items due to rations, and difficulty in obtaining manufacturing parts to repair or build attractions.

Following World War II, the park's attendance steadily rose until about 1948 when it leveled off for some time. New rides were constructed around the carrousel in a kiddieland area, and additional shows and an expanded park were added to make way for the increase in guests. In 1950, hurricanes with 108 mph gusts destroyed the park's two flagship (wooden) roller coasters, which ended up costing $100,000 to rebuild the attractions on top of the $125,000 in other damages around the park. When the park reopened for the season in 1964, a group of about 400 teenagers tore through the park destroying everything in their path, and stealing merchandise, food, and prizes from the midway games. When they left the park they broke windows and caused panic in homes in the nearby neighborhood. This random act of violence and vandalism made attendance slow that year, resulting in limited funds for the rest of the summer.

At the close of that season, the owners announced that the park would not reopen, and that even if the deal to sell it to a realty company (which planned on putting apartments there) did not go through, the park would remain closed. The sale did not go through, and Olympic Park remained closed for the next 13 years, while all of the remaining rides were gradually sold off and refurbished for use in other parks.

The carrousel Disney purchased, at about 60 feet in diameter, is one of the largest ever created by the Philadelphia Toboggan Company. The company constructed 89 carrousels prior to the Great Depression. Of the 89, Disney's carrousel is number 46, and it is believed to be one of only about a dozen left in one piece. As you may imagine, given the unfortunate end of Olympic Park, the carrousel underwent an extensive refurbishment before opening to guests in the Magic Kingdom. As part of the refurbishment, the attraction was given a more royal appearance in contrast to its prior classic color scheme. Twenty-three karat gold leaf was added to the designs of the horses, making the carrousel more valuable than any of its previous owners would have ever imagined.

Toad Ins

One of the strangest protests in the history of American popular culture took place in the Magic Kingdom's Fantasyland near what is now the Many Adventures of Winnie the Pooh attraction. When it was announced that the space's previous occupant, Mr. Toad's Wild Ride, would be closing to make way for a Winnie the Pooh, some fans lost it. T-shirts were created, petitions signed, and actual protests took place to convey the message that Mr. Toad should stay in Fantasyland.

A committed group of fans took to the streets, or the Magic Kingdom, donning the same Mr. Toad shirts and raising awareness and support for their beloved attraction. The reasoning behind the protests was that some fans felt that the company was replacing a classic attraction with Winnie the Pooh, which they saw as the "next big thing." The "next big thing" is how the Toad-supporters described the takeover when speaking with reporters from the *Orlando Sentinel* and on their own website, SaveToad.com. Winnie the Pooh's fanbase goes much further back than 1997, though, so make of that what you will. I recommend looking up the Toad Ins website, as even though I was a huge fan of Mr. Toad, I find the website quite humorous to look at today.

The drama that ensued over the closure was astonishing. Supporters of Toad regularly spent hours camping out by the attraction, wearing shirts that read "Ask me why Mickey is killing Mr. Toad" as a way of garnering awareness for the importance of the attraction. During some of the larger Toad Ins, Disney assigned extra security staff members in Fantasyland to accommodate the crowds. To demonstrate how popular the protests against Winnie the Pooh were, consider that over 600 Save Toad shirts were sold, and over 1,500 people subscribed to the Save Toad mailing list. Protesters even claim to have distributed 13,000 Save Toad postcards.

The press turnout for the protests was also mind-boggling. It seems that every news outlet from CNN to the *New York Times* had some sort of coverage of the Toad Ins. On the final day of Mr. Toad's operation, news crews interviewed fans who had flown in and driven from all over the country to give the attraction a final send-off. It is believed that about 100 green shirt-clad fans were in Fantasyland supporting the attraction right down to its final ride.

The Toad Ins represent an interesting time period in Disney history, and in American history in general, as we think about the way that social media has changed situations like this one. The entire Toad situation began when Jef Moscot, a student at the University of Miami, heard from an "inside source" that the ride would be closing to make way for Winnie the Pooh. (Though Jef has not confirmed what the source was, a logical guess might be a student from his university who worked in the park during a Disney College Program season.) Regardless of the source, the point here is that it was not (at least in the beginning) officially confirmed by Disney. All the protests and fanfare were the result of one person's tip and hundreds of other hunches. When Jef started SaveToad.com, the movement began—though certainly in a much different way than it would happen now.

By September 1998, Disney had officially announced the closure of Mr. Toad's Wild Ride. The protesters were outraged, and continued to hold Toad Ins through the last day of operation on September 7, 1998. Reportedly, t-shirts were even sold at the park unofficially by Jef during the final Toad Ins, in a frenzy that took place so quickly Disney cast members were unable to stop it.

The closure of Mr. Toad's Wild Ride and the craziness that ensued shows the clear change in how social media is used when announcing important decisions like this one. Disney has since learned from this experience, and would never announce that an attraction is closing within days of the last ride or show. The last-minute announcement for Mr. Toad caused total chaos as fans traveled from across the country (and some even from other countries) to have one last ride before Toad was "dead" for good. If an attraction closes today, Disney would announce it officially on the Disney Parks Blog, and fans would have at least a couple of weeks if not months to make their way to the parks if they so wanted to. The 1990s were a different time, however. There was no immediate gratification to simply check Facebook or Twitter and see hundreds of sources confirming the closure of a ride. Instead, guests learned most information by word of mouth, and were only able to share the information via email lists and websites (that would be considered crude compared to today's web design standards).

Mr. Toad was my favorite ride as a kid. As I grew older, I never enjoyed Winnie the Pooh, at least not as much as other kids my age probably did, because I remembered him as the character who took away my favorite ride. I even remember refusing to ride Pooh when we visited the Magic Kingdom the following year, probably much to the bewilderment of my family who hadn't followed the Toad Ins as well as I had.

Mr. Toad is still seen in the Many Adventures of Winnie the Pooh, where he is shown giving the deed to the attraction space to Owl, and another one of the original characters,

Moley, is also seen in an image alongside Pooh. On the more morbid side, and ironic given the "Pooh/Mickey is killing Toad" language of the Toad Ins, a statue of Toad can be found in the pet cemetery outside of the Haunted Mansion.

"it's a small world"

This classic Disney attraction debuted alongside the Carousel of Progress and Great Moments with Mr. Lincoln during the 1964 New York World's Fair. The attraction was featured as part of the UNICEF pavilion, where audiences were treated to the artwork of Mary Blair and music by the Sherman Brothers while learning that "it's a small world after all." Disney art director Mary Blair designed the dolls and scenery for the attraction alongside Alice Davis, the wife of Imagineer Marc Davis, who designed the costumes for the dolls. Blaine Gibson was responsible for sculpting the dolls, and Imagineer Rolly Crump worked on the accessories and toys that surrounded the dolls in each scene. Though not involved with the construction of Walt Disney World's version of "it's a small world," Disneyland's version was manufactured by Arrow Development, the same manufacturer responsible for the construction of Space Mountain.

Today, the attraction's song is one of the most well-known not only among Disney fans, but also in popular culture in general. What fans often fail to realize is that the Sherman Brothers were influenced by current events like the Cuban Missile Crisis while working on the song. It was 1962 when the United States was caught up in a 13-day military confrontation as a result of Soviet missiles that were installed a mere 90 miles away, in Cuba. President John F. Kennedy relayed to the American public on October 22, 1962, that the U.S. would enforce a naval blockade surrounding Cuba, and should a further threat to national security be revealed there would be no hesitation to take military action. Americans today know that the outcome of the Cuban Missile Crisis avoided potential global annihilation when Soviet leader Nikita Khrushchev put an offer on the table to remove the missiles in exchange for the U.S. agreement that the country would not invade Cuba.

With the Sherman Brothers tasked at creating a song for an internationally celebratory boat ride while these events were unfolding, they were inspired to use the song to promote peace among the different nations. Americans in 1962 were becoming increasingly concerned over hostile relations with communist nations, and while the world was on the verge of what could have become a nuclear war, the Sherman Brothers used the attraction to give a message of hope. Under the context of blending current events with the attraction's theme, the song was originally presented to Walt as a ballad. Walt enjoyed the lyrics, but he found the ballad to be a bit slow and perhaps downtrodden, especially given the inspiration, and so he requested that the two come up with a more upbeat rhythm which helped produce the version of the song we hear in the Magic Kingdom today.

Storybook Circus

Storybook Circus is the latest land to be included in this area of the Magic Kingdom, following most the demise of Mickey's Toontown Fair, and the earlier Mickey's Birthdayland and Mickey's Starland. Today, the area serves as a depiction of the classic 1940s American traveling circus, much like what we see when we watch *Dumbo*. As with many lands in the park, Storybook Circus is highly romanticized in comparison to what an authentic 1940s circus would be like as the park (hopefully, anyway) does not have unruly drunks, animal abuse by circus workers, and the occasional shifty character looking to make a quick buck. Negative sides of the classic traveling circus aside, Storybook Circus is a fun experience.

The one nod to American history found in Storybook Circus is found with Goofy's plane. The plane design used to create the Barnstormer attraction is likely based on Stearman/Model 75 World War II era trainer plane. Of course the cartoony appearance of the attraction may make it difficult to decipher if this is the case, but given the time period it is entirely possible that this was the inspiration. When the war ended, the remaining planes that at that point had little or no use were often given to stunt pilots to use in shows and in barnstorming, so this particular model may have been in the back of the Imagineers' minds while designing the ride.

While the rest of the details hidden throughout the area do not necessarily relate to any specifics in American history, they do serve as references to bits and pieces of Disney history. Many of the numbers strewn about on the carts in the area are references to various years of importance within the Disney company, mostly with respect to when theme parks opened or when characters debuted. Take a look at some of the numbers in Storybook Circus next time you visit and see if you can piece together what the references might be.

Another notable detail is the mention of "Carolwood Park" on some of the land's posters, in reference to Walt's Carolwood Pacific backyard railroad. "Carolwood Park" can also be read on the sign for the entrance to the Fantasyland station of the Walt Disney World Railroad.

CHAPTER SEVEN

Epcot

Epcot was never intended to be a theme park at all. Walt Disney's vision for EPCOT, or Experimental Prototype Community of Tomorrow, was a concept for a planned city that would use his company's ingenuity along with the talents found within American industry to solve the problems that were prevalent in our cities at the time. Walt hoped that everything from air pollution to rush-hour traffic would all be solved under his ideas for a planned community.

After Walt's death in 1966, the original Epcot concept was put aside while the rest of the company worked to open the Magic Kingdom. When the time was right, the Imagineers and Disney executives agreed that Walt's idea should come to fruition in his honor. Even without the planned community aspect of the project, Imagineers were able to take many of Walt's initial plans and use them not only in Epcot, but around the rest of Disney World (in the case of projects like the monorail and the PeopleMover). Following Walt's dream, Epcot takes the concepts of a permanent world's fair, along with modern uses of technology, to form one of the most interesting celebrations of America.

> To all who come to this Place of Joy,
> Hope and Friendship
> WELCOME
>
> Epcot is inspired by Walt Disney's creative vision. Here, human achievements are celebrated through imagination, wonders of enterprise and concepts of a future that promises new and exciting benefits for all.
>
> May EPCOT Center entertain, inform and inspire and, above all, may it instill a new sense of belief and pride in man's ability to shape a world that offers hope to people everywhere.
>
> —E. Cardon Walker, Chairman and CEO, October 24, 1982

Spaceship Earth

That's not a giant golf ball—it's Spaceship Earth. This magnificent geodesic sphere is 180 feet tall, measures 165 feet in diameter, holds 2.2 million feet of cubic space, and has an exterior surface diameter of 150,000 feet. Spaceship Earth weighs 16 million pounds, which aside from the obvious wow factor is the most the attraction could possibly weigh. During the initial design of the track for Spaceship Earth, the ride was going to continue farther along the highest part of the sphere before returning for the descent. When constructing the ride, however, Imagineers realized the additional track was putting too much weight on the ride and it would not be supported properly. Even without the extra track, the building's frame is supported today by large beams that go about 100 feet into the ground.

The outside of Spaceship Earth is covered in triangular panels, 11,324 of them to be exact. The material used to create the outside of the sphere was a difficult decision on the part of the Imagineers, as it needs to be able to last a long time while also withstanding the various kinds of weather that come to central Florida. The final material chosen was alucabond, a part carbon/part aluminum compound able to withstand extreme weather conditions. Speaking of extreme weather conditions, when it rains (which happens a lot in central Florida) the sphere has an internal collection system that collects the water that would otherwise slide off onto the ground, and recycles it in World Showcase Lagoon.

Epcot's park icon is also one of the park's greatest attractions. Spaceship Earth takes guests through the history of human communication on a slow-moving, Omnimover journey. This attraction, as the name suggests, covers the entire world's history of communication, not just the United States. With such broad overviews of concepts there are no startling inaccuracies here, but like many Disney attractions there are plenty of little-known facts and trivia hidden beneath the surface.

Connections to Ray Bradbury

Acclaimed writer Ray Bradbury was involved in the design and script-writing stages of creating Spaceship Earth. Since the script has undergone a couple of revisions since then, one of the best ways to get a glimpse of his work on the attraction now is the mural that is located to the right of the queue where guests enter the show building. Though painted by Imagineers, the mural was designed by Bradbury, as he mapped out where each figure would go and how the overall layout would look, with the goal of representing the parts of the history of communication that were displayed in the attraction.

Bradbury has other connections to Disney as well. Like the Disney company, he had contributed work to the 1964 New York World's Fair. His piece in the Fair was a script he wrote for the United States pavilion that recounted the history of the country in only 18 minutes.

Another connection between Bradbury and Disney was his close friendship with Walt that developed in the early 1960s. While Walt was working on early plans for Epcot, Bradbury told him that he should consider running for mayor of Los Angeles. He felt that Walt was one of the few if not the only person who would adequately understand how the city should operate. Walt said that he could not see himself running for an elected position when he was already the leader of his company, and had recently begun operating Disneyland, which Bradbury understood but noted that his smooth operation of both the rest of the company and the park were simply further evidence that he would be a welcome addition to the local government.

Bradbury felt that the Disney parks were goals that cities could aspire to be like in the future. In 1982, during an interview for *OMNI* magazine, he said,

> Everyone in the world will come to these gates. Why? Because they want to look at the world of the future. They want to see how to make better human beings. That's what the whole thing is about. The cynics are already here and they're terrifying one another. What Disney is doing is showing the world that there are alternative ways to do things that can make us all happy. If we can borrow some of the concepts of Disneyland and Disney World and Epcot, then indeed the world can be a better place.

Though written by Marty Sklar, the video footage of Walt announcing his plans for EPCOT show his interest in creating a planned city, and how even though he acted humble about his ideas, he was determined to create a city that would solve many of the problems that plagued towns and cities during his lifetime. In the video, Walt explains that by gathering some of the most knowledgeable people in needed industries and working closely with American companies, he would be able to succeed in creating a successful planned city.

> We don't presume to know all the answers. In fact, we're counting on the co-operation of American industry to provide their best thinking during the planning of our experimental prototype community of tomorrow. And most important of all, when EPCOT has become a reality and we find the need for technologies that don't even exist today, it's our hope that EPCOT will stimulate American industry to develop new solutions that will meet the needs of the people expressed right here in this experimental community.
>
> —Walt Disney

Presidents and Other Tributes

With a show that uses 44 audio-animatronics figures, it makes sense that the structures of the figures from the Hall of Presidents are occasionally reused. Many such duplicates can be found within Spaceship Earth. A personal favorite of mine is President Taft hiding out as an Egyptian official near the beginning of the ride, but a close look at the figures' faces and you may be able to spot some others as well. Also in Epcot is Lyndon B. Johnson, hiding behind the wheel of the truck in Test Track that guests encounter before going around the loop outside.

The later scene in the ride showing the newspapers being printed use a number of moving parts from machinery authentic to the time period, and the newspapers themselves show a real front page from the day the Civil War ended. When the machinery in the scene is not functional, it usually means that maintenance is waiting for a part. Since the parts are not regularly made anymore, it can take some time to track them down. Many of the items in the telegraph scene to the right also include authentic antiques—even the phone atop the desk, which actually works and is used by cast members if needed while the ride is closed to guests.

    As the ride vehicle approaches the family sitting around the TV in a living room, riders will quickly realize that they are watching the moon landing. Everything in this scene, from the clothes and hairstyles of the family, to the Mouse Trap board game, is authentic to 1969. Most of the records on the floor next to the TV set are from 1969 as well, though some are later and the record visible to guests in the front gets switched around by cast members fairly often. When this scene was first designed, a full moon was seen from the window of the family's living room, but it was removed when Imagineers did some research and came to realize that there was not a full moon on that evening after all.

    The computers shown in the next scene that are "as big as a house" are manned by two animatronics, an unnamed male figure and the stylish "Foxy Brown." Foxy is an interesting animatronic in that she was originally a representation of a white woman, but Imagineers later changed her appearance and made her black instead, perhaps because there are so few black animatronics in the parks. (The only black animatronics are Foxy Brown, the men at the gas station and Frederick Douglass in the American Adventure, and President Barack Obama in the Hall of Presidents.)

    The smaller computer the man in the next scene is working on is a tribute to all of the minds responsible for creating the computer as we know it today. Though guests often take the figure to be either Steve Jobs or Steve Wozniak, the official story is that the man shown is a representation of anyone who had a hand in the creation of the personal home computer. Another interesting fact about this scene is the poster of The Doors hanging behind the computer desk. This part of the ride was originally going to feature some of the band's music, but Disney was not granted the rights to any of their songs, so the futuristic music from earlier continues instead.

CHAPTER EIGHT

The American Adventure

The American Adventure is considered the host pavilion at Epcot's World Showcase, a decision that was made early on in the design of Epcot, or as it was originally known, EPCOT Center. The two concepts that make up the Epcot we see today were initially going to work as plans for two separate parks. Plans were being made for a World's Fair of sorts, with cultural exhibitions, dining, shopping, and shows, while at the same time plans were in the works for a Future World concept that would translate some of Walt's ideas for Epcot as a planned city into a working theme park. Imagineers literally pushed models of the two concepts together, creating the Epcot we know today made up of World Showcase and Future World.

Once it was decided that the two concepts would work together as one park, the next step was to name the American Adventure the host pavilion of World Showcase. In the early stages of the park's design, one concept featured the American Adventure pavilion bridging the gap between World Showcase and Future World, somewhere in the neighborhood of where the shops between Mexico and Canada are today. At first many of the Imagineers were in agreement about the pavilion's positioning at the entrance to World Showcase, but the more they thought about it, the more they decided that it may come across as elitist to have the host pavilion be the first country that guests see. The more welcoming solution, then, led to the location of the American Adventure where we see it today—directly across the lagoon from the entrance to World Showcase about halfway around, right between Italy and Japan.

Early concepts also based the building around an entirely different design. The original structure would have been a more modern, circular building that would have fit in better with Future World. The original concept would have lifted the building up on stilts, and was inspired by buildings like the Hirshhorn Museum in Washington D.C. While in theory any kind of American architecture, be it modern or not, would "work" in representing the country, it would have made the American Adventure stand out as the only futuristic or at least contemporary building in an area filled with historical representations of nearly a dozen other nations.

The American Adventure building that actually came to be is a representation of a typical American town hall, with no reference to any one specific place. Though not based on any one particular building, it is of Georgian architectural style and it does borrow elements from other historic buildings like Independence Hall in Philadelphia and Thomas Jefferson's Monticello. The bricks on the exterior were all hand made out of Georgia red clay and put into place (all 110,000 of them), and the façade uses a reverse forced perspective to make the building look taller while still appearing to be inviting and not foreboding as a building that towers over us can sometimes feel. Imagineers did not want the building to appear much more opulent than the others seen in World Showcase, and while displaying it as a sort of grand mansion, the goal was to still have the design feel homey and welcoming to guests.

Inside the building, guests are welcomed into a beautiful rotunda that features classical architecture along with quotes by noteworthy Americans and Imagineer-original paintings of various events in the country's history. Not to be missed in this area is the small museum exhibit located to the right of the entrance to the theater.

Before entering the theater for the American Adventure, guests are often treated to a performance by the Voices of Liberty, an a cappella group specializing in American folk songs. The Voices of Liberty include some of the most talented singers in their field, and their preshow for the American Adventure is always a treat to see. Representing a couple of different time periods in terms of their costumes, and hundreds of years of history in the variety of songs they perform, the group is the perfect fit for a show that attempts to squeeze all of a nation's history into just 28 minutes.

From the rotunda, guests pass through the Hall of Flags, which features 43 flags that represent different times and places within American history. The hall originally included 44 flags, until the controversial Confederate flag was removed. The Confederate flag that was initially on display was the final design for the official flag of the Confederate States of America, which differs in appearance from the more commonly seen flag with the full-red background (which was actually the battle flag of the Army of Northern Virginia). This flag gained unfortunate popularity when the Ku Klux Klan began using it in the early 20th century. The Confederate flag formerly hung in the Hall of Flags features a small image of the battle flag in one corner, with a red strip on the opposite end and a white background. The flag was removed from Epcot on the same day in 2015 that the South Carolina statehouse removed its Confederate flag, following a tragic massacre at a primarily black Christian church by a white supremacist who was known to pose for photos using the flag as a symbol of hatred.

The remaining flags in the hall range from colonial versions of our current American flag, to flags that once represented territories, and some flags from when foreign powers held land in the United States. In order of the year each was adopted, the rest of the flags in the hall include: Spanish Bourbon Flag (1513), King George III's Flag (1607), New Sweden (1638), Dutch West India Company (1655), Bedford Flag (1690), French Ensign (1700), Russian-American Company (1700), Colonial Jack (1701), Stamp Act Protest Flag (1774), Taunton Flag (1774), Army Commander in Chief's Flag (1775), Connecticut Second Regiment (1776), Continental Colors (1776), First Moultrie Flag (1776), Green Mountain Boys (1776), Massachusetts Navy Flag (1776), Navy Commander in Chief's Flag (1776), Washington's Life Guards Flag (1776), White Plains Flag (1776), Betsy Ross Flag (1777), First Navy Flag (1777), Bucks of America (1777), New Hampshire Second Regiment (1777), New York Third Regiment (1777), Tri-Color (1789), Whiskey Rebellion Flag (1794), Star Spangled Banner

(1795), Hawaiian Royal Flag (1800), Mexico (1800), Perry Flag (1813), Alamo Flag (1824), Texas Flag (1836), California Republic (1846), Frémont Flag (1856), Hayes Flag (1860), Stars and Bars (1861), Appomattox Courthouse Flag (1865), Fort Sumter Flag (1865), Old Glory (1865), Centennial Flag (1876), 45 Star Flag (1896), 48 Star Flag (1912), U.S. Flag (1959), and the 50 Star Flag (1960).

Guests traveling in a wheelchair would bypass the Hall of Flags, as the elevator to get to the second floor (where the theater is) is located on the other side of the rotunda. If you are using a wheelchair, and want to see the Hall of Flags, you are able to go into the hall and turn back around to use the elevator (though you'll want to let a cast member know that you just want to see the flags, as they will otherwise direct you to the elevator). If the show has enough staff to do so, you may also be able to have a cast member take you into the lower part of the Hall of Flags before or after the show.

Once inside the 1,024 seat theatre, guests are treated to one of the most technologically advanced shows at Walt Disney World. Many guests see the show as an American history-themed version of the Hall of Presidents, but the technology behind the show offers much more. The show includes audio-animatronics figures, with rear-view projections that work to make the stage seem larger than it actually is. The projections combined with the figures can make a scene like the Valley Forge landscape, with the soldiers closest to the audience and George Washington behind them, seem like the valley really does reach back farther than we know the stage does.

The audio animatronics, and all of the non-projection parts of the set for that matter, are controlled by a massive machine unofficially known as the "war wagon" that holds together each different set, wheeling it back and forth from underneath the seats in the audience out to where the stage is. During each sequence of the show, a different layer of the set will be pushed upwards, and the scene would then be coordinated with the rear-view projections and the show's audio. All of this happens multiple times per day without guests ever being able to tell that the entire show is essentially contained underneath their seats. It is made possible through the size of the stage, which at about half the size of a football field measures 130 by 50 feet. The show is also the first instance of audio animatronics having their own self-contained audio systems. Rather than having the dialogue come from one central speaker, the sounds come from the audio animatronics themselves. Another technological accomplishment in the show is the size of the rear-projection screen, which at 28 feet high by 155 feet long is the largest of its kind that has ever been used in a stage show.

The theater also features sculptures that line the sides of the seating area, each representing a different characteristic of the American Adventure. The pieces, known collectively as the Spirits of America include the Spirit of Adventure (Sailor), Sprit of Compassion (Doctor), Spirit of Discovery (Explorer), Spirit of Freedom (Pilgrim), Spirit of Heritage (Native American), Spirit of Independence (Colonial Soldier), Spirit of Individualism (Cowboy), Spirit of Innovation (Scientist), Spirit of Pioneering (Aviator), Spirit of Self-Reliance (Farmer), and Spirit of Tomorrow (Woman and Child). The sculptures are not representations of specific individuals but rather they serve as broad symbolisms for how these qualities have shaped American history, and will continue to shape our future. (While not officially recorded anywhere, guests may see the Spirit of Heritage as Sacagawea, and guests from Massachusetts may recognize that the Spirit of Adventure sculpture looks almost exactly like the Gloucester Fisherman's Memorial.)

The content of the show was built around the initial design of the theater. When the broader concept of an American history-themed attraction was suggested for the pavilion, Walt Disney Imagineering envisioned a ride-through attraction. As they began to work out more of the details of the American Adventure, it began to seem like a ride would not be the best way to portray the country's history. Part of the issue was timing. It is much easier, and safer given the ridiculous number of guests who take it upon themselves to leave ride vehicles before they return to the station, to have a lengthy show. Rides work better when they only last for a couple of minutes. One reason for this is that it is more efficient to move guests through a line and on and off a ride when the ride does not last too long. A shorter ride means that more guests will be able to experience the attraction in a given day. A theater, however, particularly one that holds just over 1,000 guests, would not have a similar problem. Even with the show occurring every 45 minutes or so, since such a large number of guests could fit into each showing, the attraction would still be running efficiently.

The Imagineers also felt that given the subjects that would be discussed in the attraction, a seated performance would be a better representation of the country's history. This point becomes particularly true when dealing with the more difficult subjects in American history, like slavery for instance. Frederick Douglass' monologue in the current American Adventure show is stirring and informs guests while also making them feel something about what they are seeing. If this scene were taking place while guests were riding by in a vehicle, so each guest could only hear about five seconds of what Douglass was saying, the point would not come across nearly as well. Additionally, having a show feature these kinds of topics does not seem as insensitive toward them as a ride would be. Though in theory there is no real reason for this to be the case, a thoughtful conclusion might be that the movement of the ride in itself exudes "fun." Whether or not the imagery around the ride vehicle is meant to be "fun" is another story, but regardless, guests go on rides in theme parks because part of the fun is moving through the attraction. A show on the other hand is something guests can do to be informed. Even with the entertainment aspect of shows like this one, the added time and setting of a dignified theater make dealing with these kinds of topics more informative without seeming to poke fun at negative parts of American history.

During the design of the pavilion, 28 minutes was determined as the running time of the show. Any shorter and Imagineers felt that the show would not be doing the history of the country justice, but any longer and guests may not be interested. (Deciphering how long an attraction should be is a difficult concept. Guests tend to complain when a ride feels "short" but become bored when a show is "long." Additionally, with most guests spending one week or less in the parks, it is impossible for them to do everything in one trip, and as a result many guests prefer that shows do not go on for over 30 minutes, feeling that it will take up too much of their time.)

Twenty-eight minutes, though perhaps long for a show in a theme park, is not nearly enough time to display the entirety of American history. The Imagineers were then tasked with coming up with a storyline that would give an adequate overview of the history of the United States without "dumbing down" broad concepts or giving inaccurate information.

In deciding which parts of American history to feature in the show, the overarching goal was to tell a story that Americans grew up learning, while also remaining accurate to what actually happened, and while attempting to be as inclusive as possible by using important yet under-represented figures from the American past. The theme of the show became the concept of American "dreamers and doers," and it was decided that the show would paint a larger picture of the formation and struggles of a growing country, while focusing in on certain individuals that helped shape the nation's history.

The show begins with the narrators, Mark Twain and Benjamin Franklin, though Will Rogers was the original choice of the Imagineers. Rogers was believed to be a great fit for the narrator of the American Adventure—that is, until Imagineers began polling guests and they learned that only about 5% of the people polled knew who he was. (He is still included in the show, just in a much smaller role.)

The first part of American history featured in the show is the crossing of the *Mayflower* and the first winter that the Pilgrims spent in the New World. Though not a conclusive or detailed study into the Pilgrims, their passage from Europe, or most of the details of what the New World was really like for them, nothing in this section of the show is explicitly wrong, rather it is just exclusionary, leaving out certain parts of the story. One interesting point to note, however, is the show's use of paintings vs. photographs. While some of the later themes include photographs that portray a certain time frame but were re-taken by Disney Imagineers, any time period in the show before cameras were widely used features paintings instead.

Though this retelling of the Pilgrims' passage and first months in the New World does leave a lot out (Native American encounters), it does do a fair job of reminding non-history-savvy guests about other details they may not remember from history class. The opening song and the imagery in the paintings shown does an adequate job of explaining all of the factors that the pilgrims had working against their odds of survival. Shown are the tight spaces on the *Mayflower* where far too many people stayed during the passage, along with images of the harsh reality of the first winter in a wilderness.

The one glaring inaccuracy in the American Adventure's retelling of the Pilgrims' story? Though it is never explicitly said, the show implies that the Pilgrims left Europe in search of religious freedom, but this is only part of the story. Pilgrims were separatists, who just as it sounds wanted to separate from the church of England and practice their religious beliefs as they saw fit. To do so, they first went to Holland before venturing to the New World. Life in Holland for the Pilgrims wasn't half bad, at least in terms of their ability to practice their religion freely. The problem with Holland was twofold— many of the Pilgrims felt that they were losing track of their British identities by being immersed in the culture of another country, and they had a difficult time finding jobs and earning livings there, prompting them to settle in the New World. Therefore, to be technical, the Pilgrims did not come to the colonies in search of religious freedom—they left Britain in search of it, and went to Holland. As frustrating as it can be to see details like this left out of the narrative, the show is already bordering on being a half-hour long, so having to cut out certain details is understandable.

Next the show moves toward the American Revolution, skipping other well-known events like King Phillip's War and the Salem Witch Trials presumably for the sake of time. This scene opens with a painting of colonists who are, according to the audio, discussing the tax on tea. The first inaccuracy here is intentional to accommodate the different levels of understanding of American history that various guests have.

When the colonists are speaking with one another, one man says "The British think it's fools we be!" In reality, a colonist would not have referred to the people back in Britain as "the British." The United States did not yet exist, and while the colonists were located on a different continent, they were still British. When discussing a British soldier, a colonist would have said "redcoat," "lobster-back," or "regular," and when discussing other colonists who supported the crown and were against separation, they would have called them "loyalists" or "Tories." These terms are often misused, particularly when the American Revolution is taught to younger school children, which though understandable to avoid having kids feel bogged down with the details is equally frustrating for them when they get to high school or college and learn all of the things that their previous history textbooks were wrong about. In the context of a show at Epcot, the language used is meant to be easy for lots of people to understand. Someone who doesn't know many details of the American Revolution, or a guest from a different country (besides the U.K.), may not be familiar with the correct terms, so using the incorrect but more widely known term might be the best way to handle it. The show could provide the background information for words like this, but part of the show's success is the storytelling that comes across as more of a show than a historical lecture.

Ben Franklin narrates, "First we spoke out with our voices, then we spoke out with action," while a painting of the *Dartmouth* during the Boston Tea Party is seen in the projection. Though not shown, Ben's mention of speaking out with [their] voices may be a reference to the tea tax debates that led to the Boston Tea Party. During one of the debates, the colonists suggested that Francis Roche (who owned the *Dartmouth*) bring his ship back to Britain with the tea still on board.. Roche was concerned that if the ship were to leave without government permission it would be fired upon by the fort at the opening of the harbor. As a result, he left Boston to travel Governor Hutchinson's estate in Milton to get permission for his ship to return to England. When the governor declined his request, Roche returned on December 16, 1773, to a meeting in progress at the Old South Meeting House to relay the news.

Meetings in the past couple of weeks leading up to that evening had featured a number of failed attempts at devising a diplomatic solution to the tea tax. With Roche's request to the governor being the one last attempt at a solution to the problem, the debates continued, with both patriots and loyalists making their case in the meeting house for what should be done next. It was late into the evening when Samuel Adams stood up and said, "This meeting can do nothing more to save the country!" The phrase was a planned cue for the Sons of Liberty to go from the Old South Meeting House to Griffin's Wharf to dump the remaining 340 chests of tea contained on the ships into the harbor. The value of the tea destroyed during the Boston Tea Party is believed to be worth about $2 million in today's currency.

A common misconception about the Boston Tea Party that is portrayed in the image of the *Dartmouth* in the American Adventure is that the Sons of Liberty were dressed as Native Americans complete with feathers and headdresses. Though they were under disguises (as this was an act of treason and they did not want to be identified) historians today do not believe that any of them were wearing feathers. Accounts from eyewitnesses that evening describe the "Indian dress" as ragged clothing, and faces covered with dirt and soot.

Following the image of the *Dartmouth*, a transparent script comes down from the ceiling which displays the Intolerable Acts (or the Coercive Acts). The document seen in the show is an expression of the actual document that was released following the Boston Tea Party. The Intolerable Acts were the Boston Port Bill, which included the closure of the harbor until the tea was paid for; the Massachusetts Government Act, which essentially removed the colony's charter and made it so that any colonial government position would be appointed by the governor, the king, or by Parliament; and the Administration of Justice Act, which resulted in the majority of colonial trials taking place in Britain. The act gave the governor the ability to move a trial to Britain if he felt a trial in the colony would not have been "fair," though this reasoning was used to move nearly all trials to the other side of the Atlantic. This act was one of the most difficult for the colonists to grapple with, as even though the people on trial would have been reimbursed for their travel expenses back to Europe, they would have lost valuable income from their time away from work that would not be paid back. Additionally, many colonists were frustrated that the British soldiers involved in the Boston Massacre in 1770 had a fair trial, and felt they should be treated in the same manner.

The final act was the Quartering Act, an attempt at housing more British soldiers in the colonies. This act is often incorrectly understood as the British government forcing soldiers into the colonists' homes, though recent studies have proven this not to be the case, and the soldiers were housed (probably in close proximity to colonists) in otherwise unused buildings.

The next scene is the first time that an audio-animatronic figure has ever walked upstairs. While one leg moves more than the other if you look closely, Ben Franklin's climb up the stairs into Thomas Jefferson's loft truly is an achievement in the world of audio animatronics. To get the movement as realistic as possible, some of the Imagineers practiced walking up stairs using the cane as if they were Ben Franklin while others watched and worked on the figure's movement. Once inside the loft, Thomas Jefferson begins to read the final draft of the Declaration of Independence. The figure in the show does read off what the document actually says, but the emphasis on "all men" being created equal is important since it did not include all men, women, and children.

The show then moves on to images of various battles from the Revolutionary War. Most of the paintings guests see during this portion of the show were created during production by Disney Imagineers. Eventually we focus in on a moment between two Continental soldiers who are talking about their experiences at Valley Forge with General George Washington in the background. The decision to focus on the two seemingly ordinary soldiers rather than the more famous figure in the same scene was intentional on the part of Walt Disney Imagineering. We all too often learn about historical events only through the first-hand documents or points of view of the figures we already know. In some instances, conveying historical events using only well-known figures is the best way to do so. There are many instances where the only information available is about a person of nobility, a political figure, or just a well-known person. In general though, learning about historical events through only the more famous people involved will only give you one side of the story.

This reasoning is why it is so important that Imagineers chose to focus on the soldiers rather than on George Washington. Washington's figure is an excellent animatronic, as he sits atop his horse occasionally looking down or over at his troops, but from an educational perspective the audience will learn more hearing from the soldiers themselves, as they describe the harsh conditions in Valley Forge, even pointing out that they are lucky to have shoes where many of the other soldiers do not. The two go on to mention that many of the troops are also suffering from typhus, smallpox, dysentery, and starvation, among other hardships. A small detail that this scene leaves out is how common desertions were at Valley Forge. As conditions worsened, many soldiers took it upon themselves to leave the Continental Army and attempt to return home to their families healthy.

As the rear projection pans up from Valley Forge, and the soldiers and Washington (and a cannon) are lowered back to the mechanisms below the stage, images of different battles are presented while the song "In the Days of '76" concludes, signaling the colonial victory and the end of the Revolutionary War. Both paintings shown were made by Imagineers, one showing the Battle of Bunker Hill (which actually took place on Breeds Hill) and another showing an undisclosed naval battle. Initially, some of the Imagineers wanted to include a naval scene in the American Revolution portion of the show, but it was cut due to time constraints. With naval battles still being an important part of the Revolutionary War, the painting of a battle was created during production for the show.

"Westward bound, Dr. Franklin, to new frontiers!" shouts Mark Twain as the scenery changes from the 18th century to a more Frontierland-esque landscape. Benjamin Franklin briefly mentions Samuel Langhorne Clemens (Mark Twain) to which Twain's animatronic responds, "I like to think Mark Twain was part of all that." Aside from Twain's comments here and there about his writing or the importance of libraries, and soon a single line by Frederick Douglass, this is the most audiences will really see of him during his time in the show.

The American Adventure, like Frontierland, gives a broad overview of the American West showing vague paintings that reflect settlers plowing fields with oxen, traveling in covered wagons, and the Gold Rush. The images fade as Mark Twain points out, "Seems a whole bunch of folks found out 'we the people' didn't yet mean all the people." This quote works well in the show as a gateway into the topic of slavery, but if Twain were around to see his performance in the show he may not be thrilled with his character. Twain was a diehard abolitionist who strongly supported emancipation (and women's rights) and if he were to see the show I can only imagine him yelling at the Thomas Jefferson Animatronic that his "all men" was nowhere near close to being inclusive. Real-life Twain and real-life Franklin may not have gotten along as well as they appear to in the show had they been able to know each other. Though Franklin did eventually announce that he was against the institution of slavery, this realization did not come until late in his life—in his younger years he is known to have had two slaves himself.

At this point in the show, Frederick Douglass appears to float onto the stage using a raft, in another scene where the rear-view projection helps to add to the realism of the audio animatronic. Douglass then speaks to the audience:

> Even amidst the cricket song here along Mark Twain's beloved Mississippi, I hear the noise of chains, and the crack of the whip. Yet, there is hope, hope born from the words of Harriet Beecher Stowe. *Uncle Tom's Cabin* has given our nation a key which can unlock the slave prison to millions. Anti-slavery is no longer a thing to be prevented. It has grown too abundant to be snuffed out like a lantern.

With slavery being one of (if not the most) brutal and morally repugnant parts of American history, including it in a stage show at a family entertainment complex would be no easy feat. Simultaneously, though, if Disney were to exclude topics like slavery from the American Adventure, not only would the show be inaccurate, it would likely cause anger and disappointment among guests. Even a guest who may claim to have little knowledge of American history knows of and understands the horrors of slavery and would question its exclusion from a show aiming to cover as much of the nation's history as a half hour would allow.

In any case, Douglass' speech in the show reflects much of his abolitionist work in real life, and is most closely related to one of his speeches in particular. His 1855 *Lecture on the Anti-Slavery Movement* uses some of the rhetoric he mentions in the American Adventure in discussing how the cause of anti-slavery has grown. Consider this passage from the speech in comparison to the words spoken by his figure in the show:

> Anti-slavery is no longer a thing to be prevented. The time for prevention is past. This is great gain. When the movement was younger and weaker—when it wrought in a Boston garret to human apprehension, it might have been silently put out of the way. Things are different now. It has grown too large—its friends are too numerous—its facilities too abundant—its ramifications too extended—its power too omnipotent, to be snuffed out by the contingencies of infancy. A thousand strong men might be struck down and its ranks still be invincible. One flash from the heart-supplied intellect of Harriet Beecher Stowe could light a million camp fires in front of the imbattled hosts of slavery, which, not all the waters of the Mississippi, mingled as they are, with blood, could extinguish.

In theory, replacing the speech in the show with this speech that Douglas used as part of the Abolition movement would not interrupt the flow of the production at all. Douglas' real-life speech is much more eloquently written, and it brings out the same (if not a greater) message about the fight for emancipation than its fictional counterpart. As with many parts of the show, it was likely not included in its original form due to timing concerns. Even if the speech could be read fairly quickly, the audio animatronic (especially in 1982) might not be able to keep up with an audio track that speaks above a certain pace.

The narrative of slavery continues with the Civil War sequence that follows. The Civil War portion of the show uses imagery that focuses more on the battles and life as a soldier, from the perspective of two brothers who found themselves on opposite sides of the conflict. Where the images used in the American Revolution sequences were more focused on the functioning of the government and the colonists, the Civil War scenes are more interested in the logistics of the war, and the impact it had on American families.

The story of the Civil War in the American Adventure is told through the eyes of a family with two sons, one serving in the Union army and one in the Confederate. The family is introduced while they are taking a photo for the mother's birthday and a quick exchange between the two brothers ensues. They refer to each other as Johnny Reb (a personification of the Confederacy) and Billy Yank (a personification of the Union). The dialogue in the show moves quickly, so guests may not be aware of where these nicknames come from. They grew in popularity due to their use in political cartoons at the time, and they were also used in the title of a book written by Alexander Hunter in 1905. Hunter served in the Confederate army during the war, and like many Civil War veterans kept notes and journals of his experiences which he later published under the title *Johnny Reb & Billy Yank*.

Before taking the family photo, the mother refers to the photographer as "Mr. Brady." She is referring to Matthew Brady, the famed Civil War photographer best known for his photo-journalism of the time. His photos do not depict battles taking place because the camera technology at the time was still too new to capture motion. Early photographers needed their subjects to remain very still for their image to come through clearly. In addition to his Civil War photos, Brady photographed numerous presidents, and was responsible for the photos of Abraham Lincoln that were used in designing the five-dollar bill and the penny. Known primarily for documenting scenes of battlefields, camps, and portraits of generals and politicians, one part of his life that remains lesser known today is his post-war years.

During the war, Brady took photos that were produced on glass plates similar in function to daguerreotypes. Over the course of the war, he had created about 10,000 plates, a task which had required him to spend close to $100,000 on their production. While producing the plates, he was working under the assumption that the government would purchase them from him once the war was over. Unfortunately, by the time the war came to an end, the government had no interest in buying them, and after trying and failing to find a private collector interested in purchasing them Brady was unable to pay for his studio and went into bankruptcy. His wife's death, coupled with his financial hardships and his eventual loss of vision, made him severely depressed as he approached the end of his life. His cause of death in 1896 was eventually found out to have been kidney failure, and though his life ended on a negative note, his photography business was eventually revived by Levin Corbin Handy, one of his nephews. When Levin died, Brady's work was left to his daughters, and in 1954 the Library of Congress purchased the 10,000 plates from the girls.

The Civil War story is a turning point in the show as the rear projections finally change from paintings and drawings to photographs, keeping with the timeframe of when the camera was invented. Many of the photos in this part of the show are authentic photos from the Civil War taken by Brady. When photos that best fit the story were not available, Imagineers retook their own to fill in the blanks. Imagineer-taken photos include the shot of the Confederate brother at his camp, and the shot of the family at his funeral which was re-created and taken at the Disneyland Railroad train station in New Orleans Square.

The Civil War-themed folk song "Two Brothers" may be heard during the rest of the scene. The song was written by Irving Gordon in 1951 and has since been covered by a number of different artists. Though the lyrics do not refer to any two brothers in particular, there were many families who were divided over the two sides of the war and may have gone through a similar experience as the family in the song. The version of the song in the American Adventure is actually a couple of verses shorter than the original. The full version of the song concludes with:

> Two gals waiting by the railroad track
> Two gals waiting by the railroad track
> For their darlings to come back
> One wore blue and one wore black.
> One wore blue and one wore black
> Waiting by the railroad track.
> For their darlings to come back
> All on a beautiful morning.
> One wore blue and one wore black
> Waiting by the railroad track.

> For their darlings to come back
> All on a beautiful morning.
> All on a beautiful morning.

At the conclusion of the song, the projection features photographs of immigrants while Mark Twain's narration describes how the nation needed to be rebuilt after the Civil War and waves of immigrants, or new Americans, would help do it. This quick mention of immigrants in general is the only real mention of them anywhere in Walt Disney World.

The next scene features Chief Joseph, who again makes a contrasting speech to the show's initial premise of "all the people." Based on the surrender speech he gave in 1877, his figure in the show recites:

> Enough, enough of your words. Let your new dawn lead to the final sunset on my people's suffering. When I think of our condition, my heart is heavy. I see men of my own race treated as outlaws, or shot down like animals. I hope that all of us may be brothers, with one country around us, and one government for all. From where the sun now stands, I will fight no more, forever.

The American Adventure lets Chief Joseph's speech speak for itself, with little other context or scenery around it except for the continued theme of the exclusive nature of the phrasing, "all the people." The speech that this one is based on was spoken by Chief Joseph (and written down by an army lieutenant) on October 5, 1877. Chief Joseph's surrender came after the U.S. government had attempted to force him and the rest of the Nez Percé onto smaller reservations in Washington state at the request of white Americans who wanted access to more land.

As some Native Americans refused to abandon the (albeit larger) reservations their people had already been forced to relocate to, the government threatened to return with a cavalry ready to move them along. Chief Joseph, Looking Glass (a Nez Percé war chief), and a small group from their community refused to move, and some even went a step further, raiding the nearby camps and killing white settlers.

The raid led to the Nez Percé retreat to the east, toward states like Idaho and Wyoming, but with the goal of reaching Canada. The government cavalry eventually caught up with them, and following gruesome fighting between the two sides, the Nez Percé found themselves surrounded during a blizzard near the Canadian border. It was in this moment that Chief Joseph approached the commanders of the army to give his surrender, which actually went like this:

> I am tired of fighting. Our chiefs are killed. Looking Glass is dead. The old men are all dead. It is the young men who say "yes," or "no." He who led the young men is dead. It is cold and we have no blankets. The little children are freezing to death. My people, some of them, have run away to the hills, and have no blankets, no food. No one knows where they are, perhaps freezing to death. I want to have time to look for my children, and see how many of them I can find. Maybe I shall find them among the dead. Hear me, my chiefs! I am tired. My heart is sick and sad. From where the sun now stands I will fight no more, forever.

The differences between the two speeches are startling. Where the American Adventure's version of the speech is cautiously optimistic, the reality of the situation is that Chief Joseph was pleading to simply deal with the losses that his community had suffered. Historians have grappled with Chief Joseph's speech in the American Adventure since the show opened. His inspirational and hopeful outlook portrayed in the show is simply not realistic to history. Where other instances in the show that may not be entirely accurate have been examples of information being excluded rather than misrepresented, this is one scene that is displayed entirely wrong.

Much like slavery, which although not "wrong" is glossed over with a motivational speech by Frederick Douglass, the Chief Joseph portion of the show attempts to make a largely uncomfortable topic interesting and appropriate for all members of the audience. For Frederick Douglass, however, we can work with the assumption that most guests are at least somewhat familiar with the figure, and how after his own escape from slavery he spent much of his life writing anti-slavery pieces and working as a leading abolitionist figure. But Chief Joseph, unless this time period has recently been covered in school, may not be as recognizable a figure.

The representation of Native Americans in attractions that are mostly geared toward theme park visitors or museum-goers is always a difficult subject. Disney, in operating the show as a theme park attraction, is not alone in this respect. Institutions like the Smithsonian have even run into problems with how Native Americans are portrayed to the general public. (The Smithsonian has even had additional issues regarding which items are acceptable to have in a museum collection and which are not, given that many Native American artifacts have a spiritual meaning, and that taking them as museum pieces may be disrespectful to their culture.) Whether the time constraints of the show are again the issue here, or if Disney is really attempting to re-write this portion of history, the additional background information of what Chief Joseph and his people were going through can have a lasting impact on how we interpret this scene in the American Adventure.

 Historians (and Disney fans alike) have speculated that problems like this are all part of Disney's appeal to nostalgia, an element of visiting any part a Disney theme park that makes the experience more memorable and emotional. Some are quick to point out that Walt himself had a very idealized and nostalgic view of American history, and so it should not be surprising if this point of view has had some influence over the theme parks. The American Adventure, however, was designed so long after Walt's death, and in fact the context of the show was based around the completed construction of the theater, that this seems like a poor excuse for the rewriting of history we see with Chief Joseph. Like the general storyline goes in most Disney movies, Walt wanted his parks to exemplify the premise that good will always prevail, and it is quite possible that Imagineers were designing the American Adventure with a similar mindset despite what years of research and evidence can tell us.

 As the show continues, we are taken to Philadelphia's Exposition Hall for the Centennial of the United States. The scene opens with a rousing speech by Susan B. Anthony, which is also based on a real-life counterpart. The original speech was given by both Susan B. Anthony and Elizabeth Cady Stanton on July 4, 1876, as part of the "Women's Declaration of Independence." It was a document based on the original Declaration of Independence that was altered to fit the equalities for women that suffragists hoped for, and like the original Declaration contained signatures by its supporters. The entire

Women's Declaration of Independence is about three pages long, so for the purposes of this book we will focus only on the lines mentioned in the American Adventure. The document in its entirety may be read online through the Library of Congress. In the American Adventure version, Susan B. Anthony states:

> Woman has shown equal devotion with man to the cause of freedom. Together, they have made this country what it is. We ask justice. We ask equality be guaranteed to us and our daughters forever.

A portion of the Women's Declaration of Independence reads:

> Woman has shown equal devotion with man to the cause of freedom and has stood firmly by his side in its defense. We ask no special privileges. We ask justice, we ask equality, we ask that all civil and political rights that belong to the citizens of the US be guaranteed to us and to our daughters forever.

Unlike Chief Joseph's botched speech, Susan B. Anthony's words in the show come quite close to the words in the real-life document that this part of the show is based on. The show may even add an extra layer of interest in being able to see audio-animatronic Susan B. Anthony recite the words herself, whereas in reality the words were not spoken aloud.

The rest of this scene focuses on the industrialization that was quickly coming to the United States, with quick remarks from figures like Alexander Graham Bell and Andrew Carnegie, and references of other inventors like Thomas Edison and Elisha Otis.

From here, the show takes a turn lending a view to Teddy Roosevelt and "outspoken naturalist" John Muir as the two are seen from an overlook of what would become a part of Yosemite National Park. The two discuss how the timber industry was threatening the country's Sequoia trees that had been around for thousands of years. While the conversation here is not based on any one instance, it is likely the result of a three-night camping trip to the area that Teddy Roosevelt went on with John Muir, which resulted in the designation of the region as a protected national park.

The camping trip came about when Teddy Roosevelt met with John Muir at Yosemite National Park. Though the two hit it off quickly, Muir had been quoted as asking the president,

"When will you get over your infantile need to kill animals?" They spent the rest of the trip wandering the parks and discussing what could be done to protect the United States' natural resources, and by the end of the trip Teddy Roosevelt stated that the trip had been some of the greatest days of his life.

World War I is the next major event represented in the show, and it is the first time video footage is used. Following the same rule as the camera, video footage is not introduced during the show until the plot reaches a time when this technology was available in real life. Like some of the Civil War imagery, the footage guests see of World War I was created by Disney. Although not real footage, this scene is meant to depict Captain Eddie Rickenbacker within his Spad-3 and an unknown German in a Fokker D-7.

From World War I, the scene seamlessly transitions into a quick tribute for Charles Lindbergh in 1927. Lindbergh's part in the show is so brief (and created from actual news footage) that it is entirely accurate. Though Lindbergh, and the rest of the Lindbergh family, became an unfortunate center of controversy (be it due to the kidnapping of Lindbergh's infant son, his infidelity, or his presumed Nazi tendencies), his historic flight across the Atlantic was quite the accomplishment, and it is depicted in the show much the same way it was in real life.

With 1927 behind us, the audience typically senses what is coming next—the stock market crash and the Great Depression. The Great Depression is exhibited through a group of people sitting outside of a gas station while listening to the news on the radio. The set-up of the gas station is based on a real photograph of a Depression-era gas station that was originally featured in an issue of *Life* magazine in the 1930s. One of the men sitting outside the station begins to sing the song, "Brother, Can You Spare a Dime?" The song became well known when it was performed by Bing Crosby and Rudy Vallee, but it was originally written in 1930 for the 1932 musical production, *Americana*. The weather in this scene is also a representation of the time period. When the gas station first appears before guests, it is raining, but as the scene continues and chronologically moves farther away from the Great Depression, the weather clears up as a very subtle symbol of hope.

Franklin Delano Roosevelt is heard on the radio, and he also appears at the left side of the stage in audio-animatronic form, famously stating, "The only thing we have to fear is fear itself." The recording of FDR's voice used in the show is an actual recording of the president from his inaugural address.

Also on the radio, and then appearing at the right side of the stage, is comedian Will Rogers. His lines again are in part based on things he actually said in real life. In the American Adventure, he says:

> Yes sir, before this Depression we sure had enjoyed special blessings. But you know, it seems to me that we was a mighty cocky nation. We'd begun to believe that the height of civilization was an automobile, a radio, and a bathtub. Of course now, we're a whole lot smarter. Now Congress wants to trim down the Navy so it'll fit into the bathtub, too. You know, it seems to me like we're the only nation in the world that waits until we get into a war before we start getting ready for it.

This quote, which was recorded by Will Rogers' son, is taken with artistic liberty from an event on New Year's Eve 1930 when Rogers said:

> We was a mighty cocky nation. We originated mass production, and mass-produced everybody out of a job with our boasted labor-saving machinery. It saved labor, the very thing we are now appropriating money to get a job for. They forgot that machinery don't eat, rent houses, or buy clothes. We had begun to believe that the height of civilization was a good road, bathtub, radio, and automobile.

Rather than altering the entire speech, the basic premise stays the same in the show. The additional reference of the Navy was likely added to help the show flow into the next scene. With World War II in the background (literally), the transition needed to be a smooth one. I say "literally" because the set for the World War II scene is positioned behind the gas station this entire time. When the scene changes and the gas station drops back down below the stage, the World War II submarine is revealed.

The next chapter of the show begins again with FDR speaking over the radio as the folks at the gas station listen intently. This time, he describes the attack on Pearl Harbor in another authentic recording in which he says, "Yesterday, December 7th, 1941, a date which will live in infamy, the United States of America was suddenly and deliberately attacked." The speech is intentionally cut off as the radio turns to static after the word "attacked," but you may remember that the speech actually ended with "by naval and air forces of the Empire of Japan." The mention of Japan is not included in the American Adventure so as not to offend tourists visiting the park from Japan.

In a change from the other topics of war in the show, the World War II scene takes place during Christmas at a shipyard, where audience members get a glimpse of the kinds of work that women went into to support the war effort. One of the characters is referred to as "Rosie," a reference to Rosie the Riveter, who was the featured model in a government campaign used to entice women to work in industrial settings during labor shortages while many of the country's men were off fighting in the war.

The finale of the American Adventure includes a long list of characters in a dream-like sequence choreographed to the song "Golden Dream." ("Golden Dream" is also the name of the reproduced 18th century style ship seen in World Showcase lagoon in front of the American Adventure pavilion.) The song was written by Disney Imagineer Randy Bright and songwriter Bob Moline, and was recorded specifically for the American Adventure. Included in the finale sequence is video footage and photographs of noteworthy Americans from World War II to the present. A 2007 refurbishment resulted in the inclusion of footage of the NYC fire department at Ground Zero following the attacks on 9/11. Some of the figures included in the montage are Rosa Parks, Jackie Robinson, Albert Einstein, Elvis Presley, various other members of the armed forces, music industry, activists, scientists, artists, and of course, Walt Disney. A 2018 refurbishment added Michael Phelps, President Obama and Michelle Obama, Bill Gates, Jimmy Carter, Lebron James, Serena and Venus Williams, Beyonce, Elon Musk, Neil Degrasse Tyson, and other recent American figures. Tiger Woods and Lance Armstrong were removed.

Speaking roles in the montage include John F. Kennedy, who says: "And so my fellow Americans, ask not what your country can do for you, ask what you can do for your country. My fellow citizens of the world, ask not what American can do for you, but what together we can do for the freedom of man." Martin Luther King Jr. recites part of his "I Have a Dream" speech: "I have a dream this afternoon that the brotherhood of man will become a reality in this day." Audio from 1969 announces the successful moon landing.

Who or what is still left out of the American Adventure? Imagineers admittedly knew that it would be impossible to represent every concept, person, or event notable in American history in a 28-minute show. Before the attraction even opened, some of the designers who worked on the show had admitted failing to include more negative topics like pollution and crime in the United States. Ultimately, it was decided that if an event, even a tragic event, led to some sort of improvement in the human condition, it could be included in the show. The decision to portray negative concepts in this manner was made knowing that guests would still likely question the exclusion of certain ideas and events from the show, but the end goal was that people would walk away feeling inspired nonetheless. The hope that guests would be able to forgive Imagineers for the show excluding certain groups of people or events was something the company knew would be difficult early on. The Imagineers felt that they had reworked the show hundreds of times with different concepts, and that in keeping everything within the time allotted, there would be no way to include every single idea they would have liked to have in the show.

A historian studying the American Revolution may be outraged at the little context given for the Boston Tea Party and the lack of information aside from an image concerning the Intolerable Acts. To the historian in this field, the show may seem like an abomination of the time period, giving too little details for guests to walk away learning anything. A guest with a more basic understanding of history may see the show as a touching tribute to the country's past, and feel confident that his 28 minutes were well spent.

The show concludes with:

> "Well, Mr. Twain, what do you think of our America now?"

"I think the Founding Fathers never dreamed of an America like this."

"Of course not! We weren't dreamers, we were visionaries. That is why our Constitution withstands the rigors of time."

"Easy now, Dr. Franklin, this nation is still just a youngster, don't you know. Why, some countries have been around for 50 centuries; we're barely into our third."

"That's true. But look what we've accomplished in that tiny span of time."

"My dear doctor, earlier you found John Steinbeck so inspiring, but he also sounded this warning: 'We now face the danger, which in the past has been the most destructive to the humans: Success, plenty, comfort, and the ever-increasing leisure. No dynamic people has ever survived these dangers.'"

"I may have invented these bifocals I'm wearing, but I can assure you they are not rose-colored. Mr. Twain, the Golden Age never was the present age, but with human liberty we can fulfill the promise and meaning of America. 'To everyone a chance!' believed Thomas Wolfe. 'To all people, regardless of their birth, the right to live, to work, to be themselves, and to become whatever their visions can combine to make them. This is the promise of America.' Mr. Twain, 'tis easy to see, hard to foresee, but I foresee the American Adventure to continue a long, long time."

CHAPTER NINE

Disney's Hollywood Studios

Disney's Hollywood Studios, or Disney-MGM Studios as it was originally known, is Disney's feel-good representation of the Hollywood that never was but always will be. You don't need to hear it from me that the park is nothing like any part of Hollywood, because Disney never intended for it to be an accurate reflection of the real location. Certain parts of the park feature meticulous levels of detail (like the Chinese Theater), but in general, Hollywood Studios is a dreamscape of our sense of what we imagine Hollywood is like.

The architectural style of the turn-style (touchpoint) entrance area to Hollywood Studios is based on the 1935 Pan Pacific Auditorium in Hollywood. The architect largely responsible for the construction of the original building, Welton Becket, was also a monumental help to Walt Disney while he was setting up WED Enterprises (currently Walt Disney Imagineering). The only building at all like the Pan Pacific Auditorium still around today is the entrance to Hollywood Studios. Oddly enough, the original building was destroyed in a fire only three weeks after the park opened.

Once inside the park guests come to the Crossroads of the World, named for the building immediately in front of Hollywood Boulevard (that contains merchandise underneath) and a tower with Mickey Mouse atop a globe. The structure is based on a real-life counterpart located in Hollywood just a couple of blocks from where the Pan Pacific Auditorium stood in the early 1930s. The original Crossroads of the World was the first modern shopping mall in the United States. Though considered a "modern" style of architecture at the time, we may think of this style as more retro today. The buildings were reminiscent of nautical styles and glamorous ocean liners of the time. The design of the tower in the Hollywood Studios rendition is inspired by the beacons that would have guided sailing ships, and Mickey stands with the globe at the top to signify his up-and-coming popularity in the 1930s.

CHAPTER TEN

Hollywood Boulevard

A stroll down Hollywood Boulevard in Disney's Hollywood Studios is akin to a stroll back to the golden age of Hollywood, to a time that may have never actually existed, but we believe it did in our collective memory. The park as a whole may not represent an authentic vision of Hollywood, but that does not mean that Imagineers skimped on the details when working out specific areas of the park.

One of the first such locations that guests see upon entering the park is Sid Cahuenga's One-of-a Kind Antiques and Curios. The building's function is the simple PhotoPass center and merchandise shop that is found in one form or another in each of the Disney parks. What makes this location especially interesting is the way that guests have perceived the backstory.

As the story goes, the shop's namesake, Sid Cahuenga, was a real person who along with his wife relocated from the Midwest to Hollywood in the 1920s. The two were following their dream of moving to where the film industry was just beginning to take off. Similar to DinoLand's Chester and Hester, Sid and his wife's home pre-dated the commercial landscape that would later surround their property. As the film industry expanded, their small home on the outskirts of town was surrounded by film studios, souvenir shops, and restaurants appealing to celebrities in the film world, locals, writers, and eventually tourists. As the city grew up around them, real estate agents routinely checked in to see if the couple wanted to sell, but they would not give up their home.

Also like Chester and Hester, Sid saw an opportunity to make some money from the increasing number of tourists who were passing by his property on their way to tours of the studios and Hollywood photo ops. To cash in on the commercial Hollywood that had popped up around him, Sid cleared out a couple of rooms in the front of his home and began collecting Hollywood-themed souvenirs that he could sell to passersby. His first couple of items flew off the shelf, and soon Sid's house was filled with unique antiques and other fascinating goods he had been able to collect due to his close proximity to the film sets. He was a clever character in the way he acquired some of the merchandise as well. If a celebrity were to shop from him, he would take their payment in the form of an autographed photo instead of cash. By doing this he was able to sell the autograph for more money in the shop than the original merchandise would have been worth—making an even greater profit!

Prior to the opening of the park, Disney executives went to Hollywood to salvage Sid's home, refurbish it, and set it up in a way that would make it appear to serve its original purpose (while helping guests with their PhotoPass pictures, too). Sid Cahuenga's shop would be one of the most detailed and obscure references to old Hollywood in the park…if this story were true.

Everything I just told you is a lie—a story made up by Imagineering. Disney Imagineers designed the house that the shop is situated within at the park just prior to its opening in 1989. Though not based on a real person, the name "Sid Cahuenga" is based on real concepts (Sid being Sid Grauman of Hollywood's Grauman's Chinese Theater, and Cahuenga for Cahuenga Boulevard, a street located across from Hollywood Boulevard). The area around Cahuenga Boulevard is known primarily for the bungalow style of architecture prevalent in southern California during the 1920s.

The most interesting part of Sid's story? The fact that it isn't true. So many Disney fans fall for the longstanding rumor that this entire story is true, and that Disney really did move Sid's house from Los Angeles to Orlando. The fictional story of Sid's shop brings up an interesting point—that it has at least enough detail and level of reality for guests to take it as fact. It's a strange phenomenon for Disney to be able to make up a story, openly state that the backstory is not based in fact, and still have many guests believe it.

Even though Sid's is just a dot on the map in terms of all of the different storylines in Walt Disney World, it is compelling to think that a fictional story that guests regularly fall for actually happens. Stand outside the shop on any given day, and you'll probably hear some guest spouting off trivia about how Sid was real and the building they're looking at is his actual house. The Sid situation leaves me with two feelings on the matter. First, if Disney can execute this level of detail and storytelling in a completely made-up scenario, to the point where so many guests are convinced of its "truth," imagine what Disney could be capable of if a park was ever created that intended to immerse guests in actual locations and events from American history. And second, if the story of Sid's isn't the epitome of "the Hollywood that never was but always will be," then I don't know what is.

Across from Sid Cahuenga's shop is Oscar's Super Station, which today serves as the hub for stroller and ECV rentals within the park. The art-deco design of the building is also based on a real-world counterpart, a circa 1934 Mobil Station in Los Angeles. Other small tributes to old Hollywood architecture near the park's entrance include the light-up sign for Pluto's Toy Palace, inspired by Highland Avenue's former Dog and Cat Hospital. Keystone Clothiers, one of the main merchandise locations on Hollywood Boulevard, is based on the 1934 Morgan, Walls, and Clements building for the Owl Drug Company.

Farther up Hollywood Boulevard is the theme park version of one of the most famous Hollywood restaurants: the Brown Derby. The original Brown Derby was located on Hollywood's Wilshire Boulevard. It opened in 1926 and used the logo we see today featuring the brown hat as a reference to 1928 Democratic presidential nominee Al Smith. A second location was built in 1929 near the corner of Hollywood and Vine (which has also served as inspiration for a restaurant in Hollywood Studios).

Aside from the famous customers who used to dine at the location, the Brown Derby is most famous for inventing the Cobb Salad. The salad was invented when Robert Cobb, the restaurant's owner, had to scrape together a last-minute meal for a certain Sid Grauman (of Grauman's Chinese Theater).

Grauman's Chinese Theater stands at the end of Hollywood Boulevard behind a courtyard of authentic handprints and signatures that serve as the Disney equivalent to the site's Hollywood counterpart. Where Sid's shop is designed on false premises, Grauman's Chinese Theater is more original than the actual building in Hollywood. The exterior of the building was designed using original documents for the Hollywood Chinese Theater that had since fallen out of style due to changes in the real building's construction. Rather than base the park's version of what the building looked like in the 1980s, Disney Imagineers did their research and replicated the exterior design based on how the theater originally looked when it opened in 1927. Where original pieces needed for the design work to be complete could no longer be recovered from antiques, specialty artisans were hired to fill in the blanks, adding details to the building's lighting, chandeliers, and reliefs that make the design truly unique. The original Grauman's Chinese Theater is also important for Disney's history in that a number of Disney films held their premieres there, including *Mary Poppins* and *The Jungle Book*.

In the cement courtyard in front of Grauman's Chinese Theater, formerly the home of the Great Movie Ride, some authentic handprints (and footprints, signatures, and sometimes children's signatures) can be found, put there over the years by celebrities. Many guests today do not even notice that the handprints exist (or if they do, they assume they are replicas). When each celebrity visited the park to leave their signature and handprints, a ceremony was held just as it would be in Hollywood.

One of the best stories from the prints at the park involves Audrey Hepburn. When the Disney company reached out to her in early 1989 to leave her handprints and signature at the park, she was honored, as she did not have a block in Hollywood and no representatives from Hollywood had ever reached out to her about it. After her prints were done at the park, a representative from Hollywood contacted her about creating prints at the original Chinese Theater. When Hepburn responded to the reps in Hollywood, she declined their offer, telling them that her prints were already in Disney World.

Other handprints include Disney, Star Wars, and Muppets characters, along with celebrities like Betty White, Geena Davis, Dick Clark, Samuel L. Jackson, Billy Joel, Bette Midler,

Angela Lansbury, Dick Van Dyke, Martin Short, and John Travolta. Patrick Wayne (John Wayne's son) is also featured in the courtyard. He was an important figure in the opening of the Great Movie Ride as he and the rest of the Wayne family were consulted when Imagineers were designing the John Wayne audio animatronic in the ride.

Another Disney-created theater on Sunset Boulevard features some real Hollywood treasures. The handprints and signatures in the cement are real, some of them duplicates of the ones in front of the Chinese Theater or "back-ups" in case the original need to be replaced.

Before we leave Hollywood Boulevard, we should take a moment to recognize the fascinating statue of the cameraman, located just across from the corner of Sunset Boulevard. In front of the cameraman, there's a plaque that quotes Michael Eisner's dedication speech from the opening day of the park:

> The world you have entered is created by the Walt Disney Company and is dedicated to Hollywood—not a place on the map, but a state of mind that exists wherever people dream and wonder and imagine, a place where illusion and reality are fused by technological magic. We welcome you to a Hollywood that never was—and always will be.
>
> —Michael Eisner

The cameraman statue was erected in 1991 after being completed by a father-and-son team of sculptors, Andrea and Aldo Favilli. The younger Favilli, Andrea, began working with Walt Disney Imagineering in 1987, and soon after he and his father, Aldo, were commissioned to create a new version of a work they had previously sculpted in Burbank, California. While the cameraman is often believed to be Walt Disney, perhaps in his younger years, the sculptors have stated that he is a non-descript filmmaker meant to represent the changing times of the film industry when the switch from silent movies to talkies was just starting to take off. The Disney replica of the statue was commissioned and placed in the park in 1995, and has an additional meaning that its Burbank counterpart lacks—the Hollywood Studios statue is also meant to imply that guests are being filmed upon entering the park, as once they walk through the gates they are becoming part of the movies.

CHAPTER ELEVEN
Sunset Boulevard

Sunset Boulevard is a step (or multiple steps depending on your interpretation) forward from Hollywood Boulevard. Where Hollywood Boulevard focuses on the elegant styles of Old Hollywood, Sunset Boulevard shifts to the 1940s, where Hollywood film producers shifted their focus to keeping American spirits high during World War II. The World War II influence is especially evident in the quick-service location called Rosie's All American Café, named after Rosie the Riveter.

The Twilight Zone Tower of Terror

Disney's Hollywood Studios is filled with pop-culture history, with one of the most popular examples being the Twilight Zone Tower of Terror. *The Twilight Zone* is iconic enough that even if guests aren't familiar with the television show, they will still recognize the opening theme and some of the music, along with the host, Rod Serling. To make sure all of the details related to the show were accurate, Disney Imagineers watched 156 episodes of *The Twilight Zone* while designing the attraction.

The story of this attraction takes place on Halloween night, 1939, and the interior of the show-building leading up to the ride vehicles reflects the time. The plot is that a group of guests were checking into the hotel and boarding the elevator to attend an exclusive party on the top floor known as the Tip Top Club. While on the elevator, a thunderstorm began and a freak lightning strike impacted the side of the building, launching the guests inside into the Twilight Zone. With the regular elevator no longer operational, Disney guests experiencing the attraction are invited to "drop in" to their rooms using the maintenance service elevators through the boiler room.

The Tower of Terror's queue is so detailed with authentic antiques in the abandoned hotel setting that guests have often hailed it as Disney World's best (especially prior to the advent of interactive queues). Everything in the lobby that guests walk through is authentic to the time period, as Imagineers picked up all of the various antiques from Los Angeles auction houses.

The building is based primarily on the Biltmore Hotel in Los Angeles and the Mission Inn in Riverside, California. Both hotels offer a similar overall style with an upscale Southwestern feel to Disney's Hollywood Tower Hotel, and the two sites are both registered national historic landmarks. The two resorts have hosted a wealth of celebrities including a number of presidents, and in their early years as well as today they are considered to be top-tier luxury resorts for guests looking to surround themselves with Hollywood glamour.

Like the Haunted Mansion, rooms within Tower of Terror are purposely left dusty as to fit the theme of an abandoned hotel. The signs of the glitz and glamour of Old Hollywood are there, but they may be hidden under a layer or two of dust. Other details in the attraction include the 13 Diamond Award which hangs in the lobby, and the poster mentioning a certain *Twilight Zone* episode. The award is a nod to the AAA Diamond Award series, of which "five" would be the highest possible rating. The two hotels that the building was inspired by are both recipients of the AAA Five Diamond Award. The attraction, though based on the series as a whole, is primarily inspired by a particular episode called *It's a Good Life*. Guests entering the attraction may spot a poster for a show held within the hotel starring Anthony Fremont (the same name used for one of the characters in *It's a Good Life*).

The footage of Rod Serling guests see while in the library scene during the preshow is actual footage of Serling, also from the episode *It's a Good Life*, but the voice is that of Mark Silverman. The footage of Serling was also edited prior to the ride opening to remove the cigarette that he was originally holding from between his fingers, and if you look closely at the way he is clenching his fingers it is easy to tell that he was originally smoking in the scene.

Like many of the taller attractions at Walt Disney World, the Tower of Terror reaches 199 feet in height. Buildings that are 200 feet or taller are required by federal regulations to have a red flashing light at the top, which is why Disney's buildings typically fall just under 200 feet since the light would not fit the area's theming. Speaking of height, the tallest possible drop guests encounter is 13 stories, though the height and number of drops for each ride is chosen at random by the attraction's computer system. While dropping, the ride vehicle is also pulled down faster than gravity which causes the feeling of weightlessness.

In order to pull the elevators up and down quickly, two electric motors are located above the elevator shafts. Between the two motors, each ride vehicle is capable of covering 130 feet of track and reaching its top speed during the drops in only one-and-a-half seconds. Because of the enormity of the motor system (12 feet tall, 7 feet wide, and 35 feet long), the two parts had to be lifted into place during the building's construction using a crane

Rock 'n' Roller Coaster Starring Aerosmith

If there is one location at Sunset Boulevard that seems out of place, Rock 'n' Roller Coaster Starring Aerosmith would be it. In a park (or at least an area within the park) that is based on the Old Hollywood we know from the 1930s and 1940s, an inverted roller coaster featuring Aerosmith makes little sense. It may be for the best, but many guests do not even notice the out of place theming here—and to some extent I can't blame them.

Hollywood Studios has been going through an identity crisis since the park's name changed from Disney-MGM Studios in 2008. The primary themes that made up the park prior to this point were disappearing, as movies were no longer filmed there, the studio had finished animating films there, the Studio Backlot Tour (once the park's flagship attraction) was a shell of its former self, and the Residential Street portion of the tour, which featured false fronts of famous movie homes, had been demolished years earlier to make way for the Lights, Motors, Action! Extreme Stunt Show. Fast forward to today, and the entire Streets of America area where film shoots used to take place, including Lights, Motors, Action! has all been demolished to clear the way for the Toy Story and Star Wars-themed lands. With the addition of these lands, the park will either need to seriously change direction or find some creative way to make the two concepts fit into the theme of the "Hollywood that never was ut always will be."

Because the park has been so inconsistent with its overall mission, guests likely do not think anything of Aerosmith randomly showing up on Sunset Boulevard. For Rock 'n' Roller Coaster, and the majority of Hollywood Studios, it makes more sense to view each land as a place that was built during the days of Old Hollywood and that continues to thrive today. (This helps make sense of Rock 'n' Roller Coaster if we assume that the studio the band is filming in before they rush off to their concert was used in the 1930s/40s and revived for use only recently.)

Anyone who has ridden Rock 'n' Roller Coaster knows the story, at least as told by the preshow. Guests funnel through the recording studio where they stumble upon the band who is about to leave for a concert. Steven Tyler hesitates to leave, claiming that he doesn't want to abandon his fans who just showed up in the studio, prompting the rest of the band to join in his protests. When someone suggests that they could use some backstage passes, Tyler agrees, and the band heads off to get ready for the show. Meanwhile, the band's manager sticks around to tell guests that she called a "really fast car" out in the alley for them (where the ride launches).

The only major change to the preshow since the ride's opening has been Steven Tyler's hand when he questions what to do with the fans. The singer holds one of his hands up above his face, and in a way that was almost positively unthought of by the majority of guests, he makes the "shocker" gesture with his fingers. I (and presumably other people as well) did not even know that this gesture had a specific name until it made Disney "news" that his hand was modified to be a flat palm above his head because of the crude gesture. Without getting into raunchy details, if you've seen the pre-show prior to the gesture's removal you know that it involves the pointer finger, pinky, and thumb sticking out with the index and middle finger folded in.

Steven Tyler's fingers were filled in digitally and outstretched in 2016 to cover up the gesture, which begs the question of how long, if at all, was Disney aware of this? My best guess is that they became aware of it in recent years and were forced to grapple with the decision of if and when to remove it. Anytime Disney does anything even remotely controversial (like removing a crude hand gesture) it blows up all over social media. I'm sure more Disney fans than ever have googled "shocker" since Disney updated Steven Tyler's hand. Something tells me guests did not really notice or think about it in the preshow, but now thanks to the attention it got following the update, guests everywhere can go through life more enlightened on dirty hand gestures. To add even more humor to the situation (depending on how you look at it), Steven Tyler publicly joked about the removal of the gesture on social media.

Rock 'n' Roller Coaster represents a number of firsts within the world of Disney theme parks. It is the first roller coaster to operate using a linear induction motor launch (which sends guests from 0 to 60 mph in 2.8 seconds), and it was the first Disney attraction to include inversions, of which Rock 'n' Roller Coaster has three.

Carthay Circle Theater

Sunset Boulevard is also home to a replica of the Carthay Circle Theater, the venue where *Snow White and the Seven Dwarfs* debuted in 1937 and *Fantasia* in 1940. The original theater in Los Angeles was demolished in 1969 to make way for office space, but there are a few places where guests can get a glimpse of the building today in Hollywood Studios. The largest tribute to the theater is the exterior of the Once Upon a Time Shop on Sunset Boulevard which sells primarily children's merchandise related to whichever movie is a hit at the box office at the time.

The theater can also be spotted in a mural behind one of the booths at the Hollywood and Vine restaurant. Additionally, a relief of the mural exists on the side of the archway that leads towards Voyage of the Little Mermaid and Disney Junior Live on Stage.

While on Sunset Boulevard, you may notice that many of the other buildings are designed with a 1940s revival-style architecture. Though it works well, and there are hints of southern California scattered throughout the area (like Toluca Turkey Legs being a symbol for Toluca Lake which is near Hollywood and often used in filmmaking), most of the additional shop buildings are not designed using real-world counterparts as references.

CHAPTER TWELVE

Echo Lake

Echo Lake, located across Hollywood Boulevard from Sunset Boulevard, brings guest into the 1950s. Disney's Echo Lake is based on the man-made reservoir known as Echo Park Lake in Los Angeles near Dodger Stadium and the Silver Lake and Hollywood districts. The Echo Park neighborhood was the home of early film studios that primarily shot silent films with stars like Charlie Chaplin.

The area's noticeably southern California look that we see in the park today was inspired by the authentic style of the neighborhood. In 1868, Echo Lake was founded by the Los Angeles Canal and Reservoir Company as part of an effort to curb the runoff of rain water in the nearby rivers. By 1891, the city government began converting the area into a neighborhood park, which continued to go through updates and expansions until World War II began. After the war, the residential areas of the park began to expand, and an increase of Spanish-style architecture was seen in the growing number of suburban homes there. This style of architecture is seen in both the original park and in Hollywood Studios, where it is blended with the unique California Crazy style of architecture.

Dinosaur Gertie

One of the most noticeable signs of this style in Echo Lake is Dinosaur Gertie's Ice Cream of Extinction. Dinosaur Gertie first came onto the scene in 1914 (even pre-dating Mickey Mouse) when she was featured in an animated short produced by Winsor McKay. Though we don't hear much about Gertie today, she is an important part of animation history as film historians often consider her to be the first time an animated character showed emotion—a characteristic that would come to be called a "personality medium," and Disney cartoons would soon become known for it as well.

The California Crazy architectural style that Dinosaur Gertie exhibits was at the height of its popularity in the 1950s, though we occasionally see some leftovers of the style around today. This style was often used to design roadside attractions that used eye-catching structures (even sometimes dinosaurs) to lure drivers off the highways. The style would also be used in conveying the nature of a business, such as a giant donut atop a bakery. Occasionally, as is the case with Dinosaur Gertie's Ice Cream of Extinction, the design of the building would have nothing to do with the building's purpose. California Crazy is an interesting novelty that at least in its purposeless form may not work well today, but Gertie seems right at home next to Echo Lake at Hollywood Studios.

Another example of California Crazy architecture at Echo Lake is found at Dockside Diner. The building, designed as a large tugboat (but serving as a walk up counter-service restaurant), is based on the 1930 film *Min and Bill*. If you get a close-enough look behind the counter while ordering your food, you may catch a portrait of the characters from the film.

50s Prime Time Café

A favorite restaurant at Hollywood Studios, the 50s Prime Time Café plays more on our sense of nostalgia than it relates to any realistic aspect of the past. Whether you grew up in the 1950s, or you only know about the time period from watching reruns of classic sitcoms, the theme of a 50s family kitchen will resonate with most if not all guests. And while the restaurant really caters more to personal memories of the 1950s than a specific historical place or event, the small details around the restaurant, from the style of the appliances in the kitchens to the Sears catalogs, are worth discovering.

Most of the items guests see around the restaurant are authentic to the 1950s, as are the comfort food-inspired dishes on the menu. In addition to the fun wait staff who include guests in the story, the restaurant also focuses on the coming TV age of the time. With individual TV sets at every table, guests are treated to bits and pieces of shows authentic to the time period, including a few clips of Walt Disney and of the original *Mickey Mouse Club*.

When Hollywood Studios opened in 1989, the park had additional purposes. In addition to fulfilling Michael Eisner's dream of a theme park devoted to Hollywood and movie magic, the park allowed for live-action movies and animated features to be produced on site. The Studio Backlot Tour, which closed permanently in 2014, was the park's flagship attraction the year that it opened, taking guests on a two-hour part tram and part walking tour to learn about how movies are made. A small handful of animated films like *Lilo and Stitch* were created at the park, and there were experiences designed to show guests what went into creating the entertainment they see in TV, movies, and music.

When the name of the park changed from Disney-MGM Studios to Disney's Hollywood Studios in 2008, the end of an era for film production in the park was made official. By 2016, the Art of Animation building had closed to become the Star Wars Launch Bay in anticipation of the newly announced Star Wars-themed land, and the Streets of America, including Lights, Motors, Action! Extreme Stunt Show, was closed to make way for a Toy Story-themed expansion.

When the new lands open, it was leaked to the public that a new name for the park will be introduced as well, and presumably given what we know about the theming, a new storyline may emerge too. But we will just have to wait and see.

CHAPTER THIRTEEN
DinoLand U.S.A.

As one would imagine, a park with themed areas of Asia, Africa, and Pandora: World of Avatar, probably does not have very much to do with American history. The majority of Disney's Animal Kingdom has no connection to America whatsoever except for the possibility that the park is an Americanized vision of exotic lands—not necessarily in the way that Adventureland is a 1960s/70s white American view of different countries, but more in the fact that Animal Kingdom's Asia and Africa sections, though beautiful in their attention to detail, are idealized versions of these places. As with any re-created place in a theme park, guests are only seeing the positive aspects of these locations. A person from a village like Harambe, for instance, might visit Animal Kingdom and wonder why there seems to be no visible poverty or wildlife outside of the sole safari area. (Of course it's not the purpose of theme parks to provide these things.)

There is one part of Animal Kingdom that is influenced by the American past: DinoLand U.S.A. DinoLand is often the most overlooked area in Animal Kingdom, dismissed by many guests as a tacky, carnival-style land that has no real place in a Disney theme park. This tackiness, however, is intentional in setting the scene for the story of DinoLand. This area's purpose is not simply to place guests on carnival rides, but rather to use our interest in dinosaurs to pay tribute to classic American roadside attractions, present information on actual scientific evidence of these creatures, and to further drive home the message of conservation (that ties the entire park together) in the only land that focuses exclusively on extinction.

The story of DinoLand U.S.A. brings us to the American Midwest in in the mid-1940s, when roadside tourist attractions were half the fun of a long-distance drive. Although kitschy roadside attractions based on nearly any theme imaginable exist across the country, dinosaurs are a common thread. Where many roadside hidden gems are located off of Route 66, DinoLand U.S.A. exists in Diggs County off U.S. Highway 498. "Diggs" County is the first of many dinosaur puns guests experience on their visit to this side of the park, and "498" is a nod to the opening of Disney's Animal Kingdom in April 1998.

The first building to exist in DinoLand was a gas station, owned and operated by Chester and Hester and their family, that fulfilled the purpose of providing gas and basic necessities to travelers driving along 498. By the end of the 1940s, dinosaur fossils were discovered nearby, causing amateur and professional paleontologists, professors, graduate students, and eventually tourists to flood the area. The Dino Institute was then founded as the primary research facility for the study of dinosaurs, and with all of the students interning nearby, Chester and Hester's old fishing lodge was renovated into a cafeteria for the staff. As the Dino Institute expanded, and time travel was made possible thanks to the technological advances in the Time Rover vehicles, tours back to the age of the dinosaurs began being offered at the site. The increase in tourist visitation greatly increased funding for the Dino Institute, though it did little financially for Chester and Hester's small family business. To cash in on the profits the Dino Institute was earning, Chester and Hester transformed their gas station into a dinosaur-themed souvenir shop, and created a roadside carnival attraction in their former parking lot.

Even with the gift shop replacing the old gas station, hints of the building's original purpose are still prevalent both inside and outside the store, primarily in the old soda vending machines and gas pumps. Some of the gas pumps even display the Sinclair Oil logo, which fittingly features a green dinosaur. Though Diggs County and U.S. Highway 498 are fictionalized places made up for the park, Sinclair Oil is a real American oil company. Founded in 1916 by Harry Ford Sinclair, the Sinclair Oil Corporation began as a determined Harry worked to buy and sell small leases primarily across Oklahoma and Kansas that often yielded oil, spurring a greater reinvestment.

Before Sinclair was 30 years old, he had become a self-made millionaire and was the wealthiest person in Kansas. The timing for an up-and-coming oil refinery company could not have been better. World War I had a great impact on the oil companies, and with the recent introduction of Henry Ford's Model T, vehicles were beginning to change over from coal to oil fuel. Even more important for Sinclair's profits, independent oil producers began selling off their assets at a fraction of what they were worth due to the overproduction of oil during this time.

Much of Sinclair's success came due to what other midwestern businessmen referred to as "the country boy operation," as prior to his rapid rise to success Sinclair had no technical training in the field nor had he any formal business training, but he was able to pay off the company's debts and expand substantially using his tried-and-true system of buying leases cheap and reselling when the prices went up. The Sinclair Oil Corporation is known today for its series of firsts in this field. Sinclair produced the first high-octane gasoline, was the first company to appear in racing promotions, and was the first company to offer a "modern" full-service gas station, offering amenities like auto repair services and restrooms.

By the time the Great Depression had hit in 1929, Sinclair was faced with the difficult task of keeping his company afloat while so many others around him had begun to fail. In a gamble, he took what had remained of his cash, and bought up several smaller companies that would have otherwise met their demise due to the Depression, thus saving not only the smaller companies, but also the jobs held by the workers who would have otherwise lost them.

Sinclair's style of business operations seems to fit in with the rest of Chester and Hester's Dino-Rama. Like Chester and Hester when they decided to open a tourist gift shop and carnival, Sinclair had no training or expertise in what he was planning on doing for a business—he simply saw a way to make some money for himself and (after taking a number of financial risks) went for it. The dinosaur logo was added to the company during advertising campaigns in the 1930s to spark promotions for Wellsville-refined lubricants. These lubricants were the byproducts of Pennsylvania grade crudes that were believed to have been laid down during the Mesozoic Era, thus creating the connection to dinosaurs. While a variety of dinosaurs were featured in the campaign, the most popular was the Apatosaurus, the green dinosaur seen on the logo on the gas tanks at Chester and Hester's Dinosaur Treasures. You may be thinking that the Apatosaurus looks awfully similar to another dinosaur we know as the Brontosaurus. It is still difficult for paleontologists to distinguish between the two dinosaurs, and it is unclear whether the two are one in the same or if the Brontosaurus is part of a different species. Though the Sinclair company sticks with the belief that this type of dinosaur is called Apatosaurus, the Brontosaurus is still represented in Dino-Rama just a few steps away in the midway game called Brontoscore.

Sinclair's Apatosaurus goes by the fitting name of Dino. The character proved to be so popular that the company officially registered Dino as a trademark in 1932. As with many other Disney attractions, Dino's feature in Chester and Hester's shop also brings the area a connection to a World's Fair. The 1933–34 Chicago World's Fair included an exhibit called the Century of Progress, which displayed larger-than-life Sinclair dinosaurs, created by cinematic papier-mâché animal artist P.G. Alen. Newspapers printed reports that Sinclair's dinosaurs were the "most-photographed" exhibit at the Fair, and that the dinosaurs may have been viewed by up to 79,000 guests per day. Though hailed as original works, speculation surrounded P.G. Alen's models as they appeared to be eerily similar to the dinosaurs featured in a mural by artist Charles R. Knight, which was conveniently located nearby in Chicago's Field Museum. Following the success of the Century of Progress exhibit, the Sinclair company sponsored the publishing of books on the subject, marking the first corporate sponsorship of geological education materials for use in schools and research libraries.

Sinclair's Dino (and several other dinosaurs sponsored by the company) made another appearance at the 1964 New York World's Fair, which as we know produced many great Disney attractions like the Carousel of Progress and "it's a small world." This time, the exhibit at the fair was coincidentally called Sinclair's Dinoland, and rather than papier-mâché models it featured fiberglass animatronics. The 1964 Sinclair animatronics may appear crude to us today, with their only real movement being opening and closing the dinosaurs' mouths to expose their teeth, but at the time they were awe-inspiring.

Another Sinclair Dino oddity that debuted at the 1964 World's Fair was the Mold-a-Rama Machine. For just 25 cents, guests could use these machines to sculpt (using a preset model) their very own Dino out of Sinclair's "Dinofin Plastic." Similar to the penny-press machines we see at many tourist attractions today, the Mold-a-Rama provided an inexpensive and hands-on souvenir for kids. Sinclair's Dinoland offered a useful souvenir for adults too in the form of a coupon for one free gallon of gas upon entering the exhibit. Take a look at the extra dinosaur toys floating around the upper shelves the next time you visit Chester and Hester's Dinosaur Treasures—you may even find some Mold-a-Rama Dinos hanging out there.

Sinclair's relationship with Disney isn't limited to this one shop in DinoLand U.S.A. Remember the TV series *Dinosaurs*? This Disney series produced in collaboration with Jim Henson who designed the animatronic dinosaurs on the show ran from 1991 to 1994, and used Sinclair as the surname for the main characters. Another small reference to Sinclair may be found in a number of Pixar movies, most notably in *Cars* for obvious reasons, but it is also found in *Toy Story* and *WALL-E*. Dinoco, the oil company whose sponsorship is up for grabs in the beginning of the first *Cars* film, is (like most design choices in the film) based on Sun-Oco, which fuels NASCAR cars, though the design of the logo using various dinosaurs is based on Sinclair.

As dismissive as many Disney fans are of the theming of Dino-Rama, the fact that they typically see the area as a tacky roadside carnival is just the point. Even without ever having been to a roadside dinosaur attraction, we tend to all know that they exist. Whether we have actually visited one, or we've seen one in a film, or maybe we've even just seen a brochure for one such attraction while traveling somewhere else, most Americans are familiar with some variation of the roadside dinosaur attraction. One of the closest real-life attractions in design and experience to DinoLand U.S.A. are the Cabazon dinosaurs in

Cabazon, California. Cabazon's attraction, which opened in 1975, is made up of 50 life-size dinosaurs, a fossil dig, a themed souvenir shop, and an experience that allows guests to climb up to the mouth of one of the T-Rexes. Other well-known dinosaur attractions include Prehistoric Gardens in Port Orford, Oregon, and Dinosaur Park in Rapid City, South Dakota.

While Animal Kingdom's DinoLand U.S.A. is not based exclusively on any one specific roadside attraction, there are elements that show how the design of this land was inspired by real-world counterparts. The Cabazon Dinosaur exhibit is one of probably hundreds of attractions across the country where guests can "dig" for fossils, similar to the Boneyard in DinoLand U.S.A. (In fact, Orlando's Dinosaur World offers a strikingly similar experience without even leaving the state of Florida.) Dinosaur World is part of a chain that includes parks in Florida, Kentucky, and Texas, all offering similar roadside dinosaur experiences. Prehistoric Gardens is perhaps most similar to DinoLand's Cretaceous Trail, where guests may walk down pathways and see sculpted dinosaurs in the midst of plants most closely related to the ones that were around with the dinosaurs millions of years ago. Dinosaur Park is likely the most similar, as the park was built around the area where fossils have previously (and continue to be) uncovered, and in close proximity to Mount Rushmore in order to profit from the tourists already visiting the area.

Other "Easter eggs" of note in Chester and Hester's Dinosaur Treasures include the photo of founders Chester and Hester inside the shop, the subtle "When in Florida be sure to visit Epcot" signage hanging from the ceiling by the front door, and the various hints of McDonalds colors and logos left over from the company's old sponsorship in the early days of Animal Kingdom. (Remnants of McDonalds can also be found in the queue for the DINOSAUR attraction, where pipes in the ceiling are the colors of ketchup, mayonnaise, and mustard, and on said pipes are the chemical formulas for each of those products.)

Outside, in Dino-Rama, the colorful designs and signage of the area, along with the giant concrete dinosaur looming over the park, may seem more at home near Dinosaur Gertie in Hollywood Studios. This area, however, is just Chester and

Hester's colorful grab at getting some of the profits that the Dino Institute is receiving from tourists. Primeval Whirl is Dino-Rama's answer to the DINOSAUR attraction at the Dino Institute. Where DINOSAUR allows guests to board time rovers and travel back in time, Primeval Whirl serves as a simple carnival ride along the same theme. Check out some of the details in the queue and on the ride itself if you've never noticed the time-travel part of the attraction's story before.

At the Dino Institute, the dinosaur puns continue as soon as guests are introduced to Dr. Seeker in the attraction's pre-show. Dr. Seeker's full name is Dr. Grant Seeker—get the joke? The cast members working in the Dino Institute are the interns who flooded the area to study dinosaurs when the fossils were discovered there. Restaurantosaurus, or Chester and Hester's old fishing lodge, serves as their cafeteria and recreation center. With so many Disney guests opting to skip the usual theme park food (burgers) if possible, Restaurantosaurus is full of overlooked details. A quick walkthrough will show the story of the old fishing lodge meshed with the graduate student takeover, with lofts that are now used as bedrooms, and "osaurus" added to nearly every sign by prankster students. There is also the seating area that is visible from outside the restaurant within the authentic Airstream trailer.

Before leaving DinoLand U.S.A., it is important to reflect on one last bit of theming this land has to offer: the importance of conservation. The possibility of extinction is evident throughout the land, as guests are surrounded by creatures who have not been alive for millions of years. There is one small design element that drives the reality of extinction home and connects it to our modern world. When exiting the DINOSAUR ride though the gift shop at the Dino Institute, take a look at the mural on the wall behind the photo screens. This mural depicts animals who have gone extinct, like dinosaurs, walking alongside or just behind animals that are endangered and have the possibility of going extinct, some even within our own lifetimes.

CHAPTER FOURTEEN

Magic Kingdom Area Resorts

Disney's Contemporary Resort

The Contemporary opened with the Magic Kingdom in 1971, along with Disney's Polynesian Village Resort. The Contemporary is most famous for its A-frame main tower building where the monorail passes through the Grand Canyon Concourse. The construction of the resort was unique in that the building was comprised of a steel framework and modular preconstructed rooms, designed by California architect Donald Wexler, that were lifted by crane and placed into the building. The design of the building in this manner was the result of a collaborative partnership between the Disney company and U.S. Steel, along with the architectural stylings of another California-based architect, Welton Becket. The resort originally included two garden wings located in the smaller buildings next to the main tower. The north garden wing was demolished in 2009 to make way for the Disney Vacation Club's Bay Lake Tower.

One of the most standout features of the resort's design is the mural in the Grand Canyon Concourse that was designed by Mary Blair. Though not officially named as such in the resort, Blair called the mural "Pueblo Village." The 90-foot mural is an attempt at hiding the elevator shaft that juts out from the rest of the building's walls. Welton Becket, when designing the rest of the building, had planned to encase the elevator shaft in various metals to create a more modern, more "contemporary" feel that he believed would go best with the rest of the resort.

With the various refurbishments that have taken place throughout the Contemporary over the years, Blair's mural and even the name "Grand Canyon Concourse" may seem somewhat random. When the resort first opened, each floor of the main building followed a slightly different color scheme in representation of the different earth tones found in the layers of the Grand Canyon. Though the cocktail lounge within the Grand Canyon Concourse is still called Outer Rim, when the resort opened it also included the Mesa Grande Lounge, Grand Canyon Terrace Café, and El Pueblo Room, all areas that seem more coherent with the theming of the mural. Though much more subtle, the resort does still promote an earthy sort of vibe blended with modern and contemporary influences, particularly with restaurants like The Wave and California Grill.

In designing the mural, Blair was inspired by the earthy hues of the Grand Canyon as well as Navajo artwork, prehistoric petroglyphs, and Pueblo murals. Her finished product not only dressed up the otherwise unsightly elevator shafts but also showed her raw talent. The mural featured 18,000 hand-painted, fire-glazed titles that measure about 1 foot by 1 foot from the bottom of the piece to the top of the elevator shaft. Each section of the mural features uniquely styled birds, animals, flowers, and scenery, along with Native American children.

In addition to Blair's previous work with the Disney company in various films, most notably in the design of "it's a small world," she is known in the art community for her eclectic use of color. She always strived to avoid primary colors in her work, using a more orange base for reds, and variations on the color blue like turquoise, all elements that can be seen in the Grand Canyon Concourse.

Blair's work in the Contemporary is also sometimes viewed as an artistic expression of post-war optimism. Though the United States was working through its own conflicts in Vietnam and with racial issues at home, on a global scale many artists were showing optimism for the future in their work. World War II was over, and the United States was a leading world power and manufacturer, which despite the other issues going on at the time inspired some artists that the best was still to come and that it was worthwhile to have optimism for the future.

The content of Blair's Contemporary mural with a focus on the Navajo culture and its vibrant colors is what contributes to some viewers seeing the piece as a monument to post-war optimism.

In reference to traditional Navajo beliefs, Blair has also hidden a 5-legged goat within the mural. Many Disney fans try to spot the goat while riding through the resort on the monorail or strolling through the Grand Canyon Concourse, though many do so without understanding the goat's real purpose. According to Navajo beliefs, anything man-made (in this case art) should be "purposely imperfect." They believe that only their Great Spirit is capable of perfection, and for man to create something perfect would be an insult to the Spirit. Blair followed this tradition as she had used Navajo art for the inspiration behind the mural, and created multiple goats with 4 legs, while sneaking in one goat that has 5 legs. This "purposely imperfect" goat is best seen while standing on the monorail platform (before you reach the load area) and looking up to the top, right corner of the mural.

More history, albeit not nearly as beautiful or positive, was made at the Contemporary during the 1970s. On November 17, 1973, while Richard Nixon was in the midst of the Watergate scandal, he and fellow White House representatives attended a press conference in which he famously stated, "I am not a crook." Many Americans are familiar with the Watergate scandal and this specific speech, but few know that the speech was given here. The televised Q&A session in which the president addressed 400 editors of the Associated Press has certainly gone down in history. Every president from Nixon to Barack Obama (with the exclusion of Jimmy Carter) has made a visit to Walt Disney World while in office; and though many of them gave memorable and well-thought-out speeches, none have stuck with the American psyche the same way that Nixon's has. Only a few months after the press conference at the Contemporary, Nixon became the first and only president to resign from office.

Prior to his infamous press conference at the Contemporary, Nixon had other, more positive memories with the Disney company. He was a friend of Walt's during the early years of Disneyland, and he visited the parks often while his children were young. He was also the sitting president when Walt Disney World opened in 1971, and many guests sought out the Hall of Presidents during those early visits to get a glimpse at the animatronic president. During his presidency, he bestowed a Congressional Gold Medal upon Lillian Disney to honor her late husband.

Disney's Grand Floridian Resort and Spa

The Grand Floridian is known as Walt Disney World's flagship resort. The resort opened in 1988 (as the Grand Floridian Beach Resort) and was the first Disney hotel to be noted with the "deluxe" status. The resort's theme is meant to be reminiscent of Victorian Florida, particularly of the beach resorts that would have lined the state's coast during the late 19th to early 20th centuries. Even with the Floridian theme of the resort, inspiration came from all over the country when it came to designing the building's exterior.

One source of inspiration came from the Omni Mount Washington Resort in Bretton Woods, New Hampshire. The Mount Washington Resort opened in 1902 and features a design based on Spanish Renaissance architecture. Since its opening, the resort has provided guests with luxurious amenities and has hosted various celebrities and presidents. Other inspiration comes from the other side of the country at the Hotel del Coronado in Coronado, California. Like the Mount Washington Resort, the Hotel del Coronado shares the same red-and-white color scheme, and is classified architecturally as American Victorian. The Hotel del Coronado opened slightly earlier in 1888, and also hosted a number of presidents and celebrities including Charlie Chaplin, Thomas Edison, and Whoopi Goldberg.

The closest geographical influence for the Grand Floridian is the Belleview-Biltmore Hotel in Belleair, Florida. The original premise of the Magic Kingdom-area hotels was that the Contemporary would serve as a sort of mirror to Tomorrowland, and the Polynesian Village Resort do the same for Adventureland, logically lining the Grand Floridian up with Main Street, U.S.A. The Grand Floridian being a mirror resort of Main Street follows suit with the Belleview influence due to the connections that both have to the railroad. The Belleview-Biltmore was planned as part of an initiative to increase tourism arriving to the Floridian west coast via railroad. Henry Plant, who had gained ownership of the land that the hotel sat on in 1893 (the same year of the World's Fair that is well represented on Main Street), designed the hotel in true Floridian beachy yet elegant fashion. Unfortunately for the Belleview-Biltmore Hotel, the business changed hands a number of times over the years, and has since been demolished save for the building's original wing. This smaller original portion of the hotel was moved in 2016, and plans are in the works to update the space into a modern boutique hotel.

The interior of the Grand Floridian is reminiscent of the time period of Main Street, though it is far more opulent. Citizens of Walt's Marceline would have been more middle-class, and had a resort like the Grand Floridian existed in vacation distance of them, most of the town would likely have stayed elsewhere. The Grand Floridian does achieve the Victorian theme, but for a mirror image of Main Street, it may come across as a bit too elegant. The type of guests who would have stayed at such a resort would have been wealthier travelers who likely would travel south by train looking for a luxurious stay at a Florida beach resort.

The Grand Floridian is accurate to the Victorian architectural theme with the exception of one notable detail. The color scheme, particularly the bright peachy tones of the interior, are much more colorful and vibrant than the colors often used in interior design during this period. A more authentic color choice would have been darker, and a bit dull and washed out for a resort that should exude happiness. While the resort as a whole takes on a lighter color, some of the artwork around the resort can give off a feel for what an authentic Victorian paint scheme would have looked like.

The bar at the Grand Floridian, located just above the lobby behind the band, is called Mizner's Lounge. The name is in reference to the architect Addison Mizner who is known in the architectural community for his work on stately Spanish Colonial Revival Florida resorts and homes, particularly in the southern portion of the state.

Another historic detail in the resort is the organ found in the first floor restaurant, 1900 Park Fare. The organ, called Big Bertha, was originally used to provide music for a carousel at a small amusement park in Grand Rapids, Michigan. Ramona Park, as it was called, was once known as the "amusement mecca of Michigan," though it was demolished in 1955 and the organs used in the carousel went into storage. The organ seen in 1900 Park Fare was discovered in 1963 by the Disney company upon which it was placed into a different storage building until an opportune setting was built for its permanent placement. Though the organ spent much of its life in American amusement parks, it was constructed in Paris, France, by Gavoli & Co. about 10 years prior to its use in Ramona Park.

Other antiques may be found in the piano in the lobby, which was salvaged from an estate sale in Georgia, and various wall hangings including original maps of Florida from 1775 to the late 1880s, roughly ending with the period when the great railroad tycoon Henry M. Flagler's railways came to prominence in the state. A walk around the lobby and the resort's second floor will also allow guests to come across vintage carnival models, and paintings by American artists ranging from the Victorian era through about the 1970s.

Shades of Green

Golf was always on the agenda as a recreational offering during the design stages for Disney World. During Walt's lifetime, when the vast acres of swampland were still referred to as the Florida Project, he had made known his intentions to include golf courses on the property. As the "Vacation Kingdom of the World," the resort needed to step up the recreational activities available to guests in order to set apart this location from Disneyland, which was at that time more of a day-trip destination.

Disney's Palm and Magnolia championship golf courses opened with the rest of the resort in 1971. The courses have been a part of a number of monumental golf moments during PGA World Tours and other championships hosted on them. One such moment outside of the sport itself involves famed golfer Arnold Palmer and the Walt Disney World monorail system.

Construction on the monorail was just coming to an end in September of 1971, around the same time that Arnold Palmer had purchased a nearby golf course. With Disney's recent move to include golf in the new resort, the company's director of marketing, Sandy Quinn, was given the responsibility of working out the details for hosting a PGA tour in the future. Though skilled in his area of expertise in marketing, Quinn was unfamiliar with golf and clueless as to how he would go about setting up a PGA event. Without in-depth knowledge of the sport, the one recognizable aspect of golf to him was Arnold Palmer, and since he was aware that the golfer was in the area he decided to set up a meeting with him to gain some insight into how the golf course and its events would operate.

The two were chatting by the Disney courses when Palmer became distracted by maintenance cast members who were in the process of loading a monorail onto the nearby beam. Fascinated with the futuristic vehicle, Palmer asked if he would be able to ride in it that day. The monorail was scheduled to go for a test run, and Quinn was able to get Palmer a ride on board, making him the first-ever passenger on the Walt Disney World monorail system.

The Disney Golf Resort opened in 1973 as a result of the need for overnight accommodations close to the two golf courses. When the park opened in 1971, a two-story club house was located where the center of the resort stands today, and wings with guest rooms were expanded from that portion of the original building. The Golf Resort had much the same features that the other Disney resorts of its time had, including pools, restaurants, bars, and recreational offerings in addition to golf. Despite the vast amenities at the resort, the general feeling among guests was it resort did not "feel" like a Disney resort. The style of the Golf Resort closely resembled a country club, which makes sense given its preference toward the golf courses that sit on the property, but not as much when compared to other elaborately themed Disney resorts. To change this perception, and in an effort to further update the resort during an expansion, the resort's name changed to the Disney Inn in 1986.

During the resort's time as the Disney Inn, the color scheme was updated slightly, and a temporary Snow White theme lingered throughout the resort, including a snack bar called the Diamond Mine. For many guests, the resort still felt small and ordinary in comparison to other Disney resorts, and the public interest in staying there was never met with the same excitement as the other resorts in the area.

Since 1994, the resort has been operated by the U.S. Department of Defense under the name Shades of Green Resort. "Shades of Green" is a reference to the different variations of the color seen on army uniforms. The change in operation and eventually in ownership of the resort came about in the early 1990s, when the Department of Defense began issuing surveys to determine where soldiers and defense officials and their families would like to have a resort. Orlando was chosen by the overwhelming majority, and so the government began leasing the resort from Disney in 1994. The Department of Defense purchased the resort outright in 1996 for the cost of $43 million, though Disney still retains ownership of the land that the resort and the golf courses are on. Though the resort is often fully booked, there is sometimes confusion among other Disney guests regarding who is eligible to stay at Shades of Green. Current active duty or retired from active duty members of the U.S. Armed Forces and Reserve, National Guard, honorably discharged veterans with 100% service-connected disability certified by the VA (Department of Veterans Affairs), current or retired Coast Guard and Department of Defense civilian employees, and Medal of Honor recipients and their families are all able to stay at the resort, though room rates and ticket prices vary based on the rank and position held.

Wilderness Lodge

Disney's Wilderness Lodge opened in 1994 as the resort's tribute to the American Northwest. The concept for the lodge was first introduced during Michael Eisner's time as CEO. It was originally announced under the name Cypress Point Lodge when Eisner announced plans in 1984 to construct three new resorts at Walt Disney World. Another original concept was the Wilderness Junction (or Buffalo Junction depending on what stage of development it was in) that would have been located between the Wilderness Lodge and the Fort Wilderness Resort and Campground.

Wilderness Junction would have featured over 500 guest rooms with nightly entertainment, shops, and unique dining experiences, all paying homage to an old-fashioned western theme. (In following that the Grand Floridian was to mirror Main Street; the Polynesian, Adventureland; and the Contemporary, Tomorrowland; it is quite possible that this original concept was devised to match Frontierland.) The idea for a multi-platform entertainment complex style resort based on a frontier setting was ultimately scrapped, though many ideas were later reused (albeit with a much different theme) during the development stages of the BoardWalk Inn.

The resort's main building that houses the lobby is based on famous western inns and resorts. The Wilderness Lodge was designed by Colorado-based architect Peter Dominik Jr. (son of former Colorado senator Peter Dominik) and a team including E. Randal Johnson, who assisted with the building's design, and Ronald D. Armstrong in management.

Dominik's style of architecture was upscale western, with nods to the American West and Native American art. While designing the Wilderness Lodge, the architect has cited the Old Faithful Inn at Yellowstone National Park, the Ahwahnee Hotel at Yosemite, Lake McDonald Lodge at Glacier National Park, and Timberline Lodge at Mount Hood, Oregon, as inspiration. Dominik's team, along with Michael Eisner and other Disney executives, spent an extensive amount of time touring various hotels around northwestern national parks to gain an authentic vision for what the resort would be like. E. Randal Johnson stated, "These visits subsequently led to extensive research on the National Park System, the great western painters, indigenous peoples and western craftsman who helped shape the American West."

As such, the Wilderness Lodge is designed with rustic wooden touches, including exposed beams, totem poles, and tributes to Native American culture in obvious instances such as the headdresses in the lobby but also hidden throughout the resort.

One of the reasons why Wilderness Lodge works so well in its given theme is the elegant blending of natural landscapes and man-made concepts using natural materials. The wooden frame could easily be mistaken for any wood-based building, but the evergreen colors mixed with the natural rock formations acting as supports help to complete the authentic look and feel of the resort as an American northwestern escape. This kind of theming also works well in making the Wilderness Lodge one of the most unique deluxe resorts at Disney World. The lobby's design draws the eye up toward a stone fireplace that reaches 82 feet in height, chandeliers based on the look of teepees, and hand-carved totem poles that tower over 50 feet high. Additionally, the lobby as a whole spans seven stories, and was constructed using 85 truckloads of lodgepole pine from Oregon and Montana.

The stone fireplace may be one of the most natural-looking elements of the resort, but it is actually man-made. The varying colors in the stone are intended to match the different layers of rock strata found throughout the Grand Canyon, though the designers understandably were not able to remove such materials from the actual landmark. To achieve an authentic look for the man-made piece, Disney consulted paleontologists who worked with designers to bring the colors in the lobby's fireplace as close to their natural counterparts as possible.

Other utilitarian pieces found around the resort are designed with the work of Thomas Molesworth in mind. Molesworth was an American furniture designer whose niche was using natural materials like rawhide and natural woods to create uniquely western pieces. He was often commissioned to design furniture for western-styled hotels, and he famously designed many of the pieces for President Eisenhower's home in Gettysburg.

The theming of the Wilderness Lodge is obvious to most guests who set foot on the property, but whether guests know of the official backstory is less clear. Much in the same way that guests visiting DinoLand U.S.A. know that they have ended up in some sort of tacky carnival sideshow but they do not know why, the majority of guests probably do not know the official story of the Wilderness Lodge.

As the story goes, a St. Louis native by the name of Colonel Ezekiel Moreland discovered a pristine valley along a creek during a journey in the northwestern region of the country.

The colonel, who had served in the War of 1812, vowed to one day return to that same valley and make a home there for himself and his daughter, Genevieve. Genevieve was an aspiring curator, and she came with her friend and travel companion Frederich Alonzo Gustaf, an up-and-coming artist interested in landscape painting. Her father, having sought inspiration from other westward-bound ventures like the journey of Lewis and Clark, attempted to travel back west to the valley with 50 other explorers in tow, though the group came face to face with a buffalo stampede, causing all but ten of the explorers to return home in fear.

Eventually, Colonel Moreland, his daughter, and Frederich Gustaf made it to the valley, and the three were able to settle there, dubbing the area Silver Creek Springs. Thanks to having recently run into money from trading valuable furs, the colonel was able to send for a crew to meet them from St. Louis to help establish a lodge in the area. Additional artists flocked to Silver Creek Springs seeking the beautiful views they came to know from Gustaf's works (hence the name of the signature restaurant at the resort being Artist Point—guests who have seen the private dining menu may notice that the menu is "courtesy of Miss Jenny," which is a reference to Genevieve Moreland).

Additional details of the story behind the Wilderness Lodge used to be distributed to guests in a newsletter called the *Silver Creek Star*. Unfortunately, the letter has not been printed in years, and cast members working at the resort today often do not know all of the details of Colonel Moreland's adventures in discovering and settling the resort. Today, the only references to these stories may be found in the few copies of the Silver Creek Star that are still in existence, and in articles by Disney historians like Jim Korkis, who work diligently to document stories like this one so that they are not lost to time.

The backstory of the Wilderness Lodge is filled with details that guests would never know of while visiting the resort. Though the theme of channeling the Pacific Northwest may be very clear, guests today without access to a decades-old newsletter would have no idea that specific characters played a role in developing the story. The storyline behind the lodge continues in the *Silver Creek Star* to describe later travelers to the area, and their relationships with Native Americans, which is undoubtedly much friendlier than a similar relationship would have been in real life.

The name "Silver Creek" lives on today primarily through the creek that appears to run through the resort. The bubbling spring by the small footbridge in the lobby is part of the creek, as is the clearly named Silver Creek Springs Pool, and the Fire Rock Geyser.

One of the most fascinating tributes to Native American culture at the lodge, and perhaps in the entire Walt Disney World Resort, is the Hopi storm pattern found on the lobby floor. Members of the Hopi tribe have historically lived throughout the western United States, though most today live in northeastern Arizona. The tribe keeps a powerful covenant with Maasaw, the ancient caretaker of the earth, and the nation seeks out peace and strives to show the utmost respect for the natural world.

In Hopi culture, storm patterns are used in various art forms to convey the tribe's relationship to the spiritual world around them. The storm pattern alludes to the belief that all living things are brought to earth by passing from the underworld to the Lake of Emergence. In the storm pattern, the Lake of Emergence is symbolized by the square or rectangular shape in the middle of the design. The lines and zig-zags that spread out from the Lake of Emergence represent lightning bolts, which direct life from the Lake of Emergence to Earth, and eventually to the four corners of the storm pattern. The four corners are symbolic of the Hopi's four sacred peaks, which include the San Francisco Peaks in Arizona, Mount Taylor in New Mexico, and Mount Hesperus and Sierra Blanca in Colorado. In the Wilderness Lodge, the peaks are represented in the pattern by the bundles of timber in the lobby's corners, which span about five stories of the resort.

Hanging above the storm pattern-designed floor are the resort's teepee-inspired chandeliers. While many Native American tribes did not actually use teepees (despite common stereotypes depicting various groups using them) the tribes represented in the Wilderness Lodge are known to have used them. Many of the nomadic Native American tribes in the

Pacific Northwest, including members of the Navajo nation which the resort's décor is based on, were known to have used teepees. The ones used to make the chandeliers at the resort are made from rawhide as their real-life counterparts would be, and they each weigh about 600 pounds. The symbols painted on the chandeliers are a blend of designs authentic to Native American culture in the region, as well as some additional cowboys on horseback.

Two totem poles mark the outskirts of the lobby, one near the front desk and the other located near Whispering Canyon Café. Like the other Native American-inspired design elements described thus far, the poles are authentic to the cultures they represent. The poles themselves are made from red cedars that are estimated to be about 400 years old. The artwork on the totem poles was done by Duane Pasco, who, although not Native American himself, is renowned as one of the best carvers in indigenous-inspired artwork. The designs on the poles are representative of two clans: the Eagle Clan (on the pole near the front desk) and the Raven clan (on the pole near the restaurant). The reasoning behind including the clans on the poles is that many northwestern Native Americans believe that their personal lineages can be traced back to one of the two clans. Though the theme of the poles fits into an authentic Native American narrative, the one obvious inaccuracy is the inclusion of the Disney characters, which was a choice made by Disney representatives, not the artist.

Other Native American details include the boards fixed on the wall behind the front desk, with each board known as a papoose. The papoose is an item used by a number of different tribes to carry a baby by attaching it to the wearer's back, like a sturdier version of the baby slings we often see parents using.

Disney takes Native American authenticity one step further by hosting ceremonies in celebration of Native American Heritage Month at the resort each November. Each year, Native American interpreters James Hansen (Black Wolf) and Anita Hansen (Quick Silver) answer questions from guests regarding their heritage, and perform a ceremony in the resort with the intention or purifying the resort for the coming year and ridding the area of negative energy.

The Disney Vacation Club Villas at the Wilderness Lodge bring us back to yet another instance of Walt Disney's love for the railroad serving as inspiration for a piece of the resort. The Disney Vacation Club (or DVC) side of the resort was not completed until the year 2000, though Imagineers worked to ensure that the storyline of the buildings made them appear older than the rest of the resort. The architecture of the villas is more inspired by the American railroad, and the diluted red hues of the buildings' rooftops are intended to make it look more aged than the main building. Where the main building is based on the inns and lodges surrounding northwestern national parks, the DVC side is meant to transport guests to an older northwestern railroad hotel. Reinforcing the railroad inspiration is the room known as the Carolwood Pacific Room, in reference to Walt's backyard railroad. The room even features two cars that were part of Walt's original train (and that were donated to the company by his daughter, Diane).

Fort Wilderness Resort and Campground

Disney's Fort Wilderness Resort and Campground is an important part of theme park history in its own right as it was one of the first strategies used to set Walt Disney World apart from its competitors. With early advertising campaigns hailing the resort as the "Vacation Kingdom of the World," additional recreational offerings needed to be constructed to live up to the hype. When Walt dreamed up the Florida Project, he did not want the new resort to be limited to a Magic Kingdom park where guests would spend the day and then return home, or to their hotel, but rather he wanted guests to be able to plan an entire vacation experience around a trip to the theme parks.

In a time when this kind of vacation destination did not yet exist, Walt was ahead of the curve. During his lifetime, amusement parks were the norm, whereas detailed *theme* parks like Disneyland were just coming to fruition. Additionally, even people who traveled to visit a theme park or similar tourist attraction spent much of their vacation doing just that. When families were done with Disneyland, for instance, they'd leave the park and visit other local tourist attractions. Understanding that there is only so much to be done in the parks, Walt planned to create an entire vacation complex that would keep guests on Disney property and coming back for more. Fort Wilderness was a vital part of this plan.

When Disney executives thought of activities that comprised best-loved family vacations, camping trips came to mind. To combine this element of family vacations with the opening of the Magic Kingdom, then operations chief Dick Nunis consulted with Keith Kambak. Kambak had a degree in recreation, which was what initially led Nunis and other executives to see him as the right man for the job, and he had also worked at Disneyland. When it was found out that Kambak had no personal experience visiting campgrounds, the Imagineers had an unexpectedly positive reaction. They felt that his lack of experience would help set Disney's campground apart from the others, and while they did send Kambak on months of research to learn about the facilities, they knew that he would not be biased toward any certain characteristics or types of campgrounds.

After overcoming internal difficulties during construction, namely that Kambak consistently lost workers on the campground project to the growing number of cast needed to work on completing the construction of the Magic Kingdom, Fort Wilderness Resort and Campground was able to open just one month after the park's opening day. Opening the area in November was not without a fight, though. In order to make up for lost resources when construction work was moved to other parts of the resort, Kambak and the other employees moved needed materials into Fort Wilderness and sometimes worked late in the evening or through the night to continue making progress on the site.

Fort Wilderness today is comprised of campsites and cabins, along with the Tri-Circle D Ranch, which houses Walt Disney World's horses, and unique dining options like the Hoop Dee Doo Musical Revue and Mickey's Backyard Barbecue. The ranch is named using "D" for Disney and Tri-Circle in reference to a simple Mickey shape made out of three circles. Following the success of the Spirit of Aloha dinner show at the Polynesian Village Resort, the Hoop Dee Doo Musical Revue opened in 1974 to celebrate old frontier-style vaudeville comedy in a family-friendly setting. The show is a fun display of classic Americana as the Pioneer Hall Players perform playful renditions of American folk music while offering comedic entertainment throughout the event. It is also known for being the longest performing musical stage show in history.

No longer at Fort Wilderness today is the Fort Wilderness Railroad, which like the Walt Disney Railroad was created out of authentic antique steam trains, and the Disney company's first waterpark, River Country. River Country was designed to fit the theme of Fort Wilderness as an "ol' swimmin' hole." The park closed in 2002 due to reasons unconfirmed by Disney, though it is speculated that the possible reasons were the discovery of a rare and deadly amoeba in the fresh (lake) water used in the park, its inconvenient location at Fort Wilderness due to the amount of time it would take non-resort guests to get there, and competition from other parks, both other Disney water parks as they were built and other Orlando waterparks. Though River Country sits largely abandoned today, and urban explorers have reached the area and taken photos that are easy to find with a quick internet search, Disney has announced plans to take down the remaining structures and completely fill in the area.

CHAPTER FIFTEEN

Epcot Area Resorts

The Epcot area resorts include Disney's Yacht and Beach Club resorts and Disney's BoardWalk Inn (and entertainment complex). If Liberty Square is the most noticeable display of American history (or at least Americana), then the Epcot resorts may be the most understated. Though most guests know that when they walk through the Yacht and Beach resorts they are meant to be wandering through a New England seaside resort, we rarely ever think of the setting at these resorts, and many of the small details that add to this story go unnoticed.

Yacht & Beach Club

Disney's Yacht Club was the first Epcot area resort to open (following the Walt Disney World Swan and Dolphin resorts, which although have "Walt Disney World" in their names are not technically Disney resorts. A corporate partnership allows for them to operate on Disney property, and guests staying there enjoy many of the same benefits as Disney resort guests.) The Yacht Club is modeled after the grand seaside resorts commonly found on Nantucket or Martha's Vineyard, while the Beach Club is designed more exclusively on Newport. Following this premise, the architect who designed the Yacht Club (and Beach Club and Boardwalk) was Robert A.M. Stern, who is known for his work on beachfront properties throughout the East Coast.

While the Yacht Club and the Beach Club are separate sister resorts, they are much more similar than different. They have the same layout and overall design with slightly different theming, in terms of the Yacht Club portraying a more upscale New England aesthetic while the Beach Club appears more laid back. The two resorts also share the highly sought-after pool area, Stormalong Bay, and they are home to popular Disney restaurants like Beaches and Cream and Yachtsman Steakhouse.

BoardWalk Inn

Disney's BoardWalk Inn is based on the Atlantic City boardwalk, in New Jersey. The BoardWalk Inn is a highly idealized interpretation of Atlantic City, as much of the riffraff (gambling rings, prostitution, public intoxication) is obviously not on display at the Disney resort. The Boardwalk may not represent the Atlantic City we see in New Jersey today, but it does harken back to an earlier time when classic boardwalks were sweeping beach towns around the United States.

Atlantic City's boardwalk is one of the first to exist in the United States. The boardwalk opened in 1870 and is still thriving today. In addition to Atlantic City, the resort takes cues from classic amusement parks like Luna Park and Coney Island, and even goes so far as to include a pool with a waterslide reminiscent of a wooden roller coaster, and a pool bar designed after a carousel. The lobby features a carousel (though miniature), and like other carousels seen at Walt Disney World this item is authentic to the time and setting of the resort and was purchased and restored by Disney.

Also in the lobby is a model of the Flip-Flap Railway. This roller coaster, which was a staple at Coney Island during its time, was the first inverted rollercoaster ever created. It opened in 1895, and featured one inverted loop that during its short time caused riders a great deal of discomfort. Since the 20th century, inverted rollercoasters were designed using teardrop-shaped loops. This is because early roller coasters with fully circular loops allowed riders to experience far too extreme levels of g-forces. Additionally, the Flip Flap Railway had no seatbelts, and so the curve of the loop often left riders with whiplash. Though the ride was only open for about seven years, it paved the way for designers to try their hand at other (safer) inverted roller coasters.

The BoardWalk Inn is full of such details, like a ballyhoo banner hanging near the entrance to the resort that during the 19th century (and even through to the present in some areas) was used in carnivals and circuses to attract guests over to a certain area. Though probably not as effective, there are ballyhoo settings on some of the automated carnival games in Animal Kingdom's DinoLand that feature light-up and musical effects in an effort to entice guests to come over and play.

The elephant above the lobby's fireplace is named Lucy, and she (along with the photo of her next to the item) is another version of the California Crazy style of architecture we see with Dinosaur Gertie in Hollywood Studios. Like many California Crazy buildings, the original elephant was constructed to grab the attention of drivers in hopes that they would stop and, in Lucy's instance, purchase real estate in Margate, New Jersey. Lucy has been around since 1882, and if you ever happen to make it to Margate the building is open to the public for tours.

CHAPTER SIXTEEN

Disney Springs Area Resorts

Port Orleans

The resorts we know today as Port Orleans: Riverside and Port Orleans: French Quarter first opened to the public in the early 1990s—French Quarter in 1991 and Riverside in 1992. When the resort opened, Riverside was not yet part of the Port Orleans resort complex, and instead it was known as Dixie Landings. Where French Quarter was inspired by the stately architecture of New Orleans' French Quarter district, Dixie Landings was based on the city's more rural outskirts. By 2001, Disney had begun reworking the idea of Dixie Landings to move the resort's theme away from the pre-Civil War years (where slavery had been alive and well, and presumably would have taken place in the setting of the resort's story given the cotton mill). The use of the word "Dixie" and some other nomenclature in Dixie Landings prompted some changes that ultimately resulted in a merger with French Quarter.

The two resorts are located along the banks of Disney's man-made Sassagoula River. This river is where guests are able to catch boats to Disney Springs, making the additional non-bus transportation feature a prime selling point for the resort. The name "Sassagoula" is also an Imagineer-created name for a river, though it comes from a Native American word for "Mississippi." The resorts were designed by Fugleberg Koch Architects, the firm also responsible for the design of Disney's Old Key West and Caribbean Beach resorts.

Old Key West

Disney's Old Key West was known as Disney's Vacation Club Resort in 1991. What has since evolved into Disney World's "best-kept secret" originally began as a fairly standard timeshare. The name Old Key West and the Key West-specific theme did not become a part of the resort until 1996. Today, the resort is available to both regular guests and members of the Disney Vacation Club. One fun hint of American history at Old Key West is the Gurgling Suitcase bar. The term "gurgling suitcase" refers to Prohibition-era suitcases that contained alcohol and were therefore smuggled from Cuba (where they were loaded up with rum) into the Florida Keys and then passed through the northern states. To quickly check if suitcases did contain liquor, police would shake the bags and listen to see if they could hear liquid sloshing around, or "gurgling."

Saratoga Springs

A later addition to the Disney Vacation Club came in 2004 with the opening of Saratoga Springs, based on the real-life counterpart in upstate New York. Before Saratoga Springs existed as a Disney Vacation Club resort, however, the Disney Institute occupied the same land. In some ways the Disney Institute was the more modern answer to Walt's interest in creating a planned city.

With this whole idea put on the backburner after Walt's death, it was not revived until the 1990s, when Michael Eisner was CEO and believed that he would be able to live up to Walt's dream. What became the Disney Institute was an expansion upon this idea that a planned community could exist at Walt Disney World. The Disney Institute was essentially a Disney "university" of sorts that would allow guests to stay on property (at what is now Saratoga Springs) and take classes in everything from marketing and design to animation and culinary offerings. Some original buildings from the Disney Institute are still standing at Saratoga Springs, though they have since been incorporated into the resort we see today, such as the building that houses the resort's quick service restaurants, and the main building where the lobby is located.

The Disney Institute closed in 2003 to make way for the resort, but many of the ideas and plans from the Institute still exist around Disney World. The living component of the institute may be translated into the contemporary communities of Celebration and Golden Oak, and while the types of classes that were offered at the Institute are for the most part no longer offered at all, we occasionally see some similar events at Epcot's festivals. The Epcot International Food and Wine Festival, for instance, usually hosts some cooking classes. Other educational opportunities may come today in the form of backstage tours and quick 20-minute animation classes. (The animation classes had previously been offered at Disney's Hollywood Studios in the Magic of Disney Animation building, along with the Art of Animation Resort; however, with the closing of the Hollywood Studios facility to make way for the Star Wars Launch Bay, the classes are currently only offered at the resort.)

The Disney Institute does exist today, albeit under an entirely different format. The brand hosts business-specific classes geared toward educating non-Disney leaders on what the Disney company does best. The courses are usually scheduled for multiple days and can take place at a convention center at Disney World or in various other locations.

CHAPTER SEVENTEEN

Everything Else

Value Resorts

It is no secret that one of the disadvantages of staying at a value resort is the less authentic theming in the resort's design. For many guests, the resort is simply a place to sleep and take a shower, and as long as the room is clean and comfortable, everything else is not as important. If the value resorts reference any time in American history, it is the nostalgic recent past. Many guests enjoy staying at Pop Century because they enjoy seeing the larger-than-life icons from their youth. The All Star Resorts (Movies, Music, and Sports) all use their respective themes to create a similar style of décor.

Disney's Art of Animation Resort may be the standout of the value resorts in terms of how they represent our collective past if for nothing else but the small details in the lobby. All of the drawings and animation stills displayed in the lobby are original pieces of artwork from their respective films that have never been displayed anywhere else.

The value resorts may not come with the same historical grandeur as, say, the BoardWalk Inn, but they do come with their own sense of nostalgia, not only for the general idea of the past but for past family vacations as well.

Disney Springs

Disney Springs is based on an important part of Florida's natural landscape that unfortunately tends to be overlooked by guests visiting Orlando. Florida has the highest amount of natural freshwater springs in the same area compared to anywhere else in the U.S. and even in the world. In fact, Florida is home to about 900 springs within one relative area, many of which are within driving distance from Walt Disney World.

Imagineers used this knowledge as a basis for re-theming Disney Springs. Previously the area had been known as Downtown Disney, and while Disney Springs serves essentially the same purpose as a dining, shopping, and entertainment complex, this change marks the first time that Imagineers have worked to give the location a coherent story.

Like most "based on a real-life location" stories around Disney World, the story of Disney Springs is that many years ago visitors came from all over to see the springs, prompting towns to settle in these areas (like Florida's Silver Springs or De Leon Springs). As more people learned about the springs, the town continued to grow and expand, attracting not only locals looking to move there but also visitors from all over the world. (Sounds kind of like Walt Disney World, doesn't it?) In addition to Florida's natural springs, Imagineers also looked to Kismet, Florida, for inspiration. Kismet was where Walt's parents were married and where they lived briefly before moving to Chicago.

Kismet no longer exists as a functioning town. The entire area has become a ghost town, with most remaining pieces of evidence for the town's previous existence being early photographs and artifacts that now belong to the Florida State Archives. The town experienced a wave of bad luck in the late 19th and early 20th centuries, causing many of its citizens to pick up and move elsewhere. A cold winter season followed by a fire that destroyed whatever remaining farms and crops the past winter had not gave the townspeople cause for concern. The town still had residents throughout the early part of the 20th century, though by the 1960s only a few people remained. By the 1970s, the town was essentially deserted and what did remain was being destroyed by vandals. During its prime, Kismet was a thriving little town that attracted settlers from the northern and midwestern states down to Florida, with distinctive neighborhoods, promises of citrus productions (and profits), and a cozy, hometown feel.

Epilogue

We've now come full circle, from Walt's vision of Marceline, Missouri, to his parents' one-time home of Kismet, Florida, with every time and place in between. Walt Disney World is based on so many specifics of American history, yet in a simultaneous state of nostalgia. Is that Walt Disney World Resort qualified in relaying American history to the general public? Maybe...and maybe not.

This qualification (in terms of a theme park, anyway) comes more with storytelling than it does in portraying accuracy. Historical accuracy is no doubt extremely important; however, particularly in such an entertainment-based environment, it is impossible to predict what guests will take away from the experience. Regardless of how accurate the details are, the average guest is going to leave at the end of the day with memories that will last a lifetime because of the experiences they had and the people they were with. Frontierland may not be 100% accurate on all accounts, but guests will take away more from having the time of their lives with friends and family in what they at least believe to be the western frontier regardless of whether or not the area is true to its name.

Whether accurate or not, the details found all over the Walt Disney World Resort can inspire guests to learn more about history even when their vacation is over. I remember the first time I watched the American Adventure show and heard the speeches by Frederick Douglass and Chief Joseph. I wanted to know if those speeches were authentic. In the pre-Google days of the 90s, I asked my family leaving the show if the speeches were real, only to be met with a wide range of answers including the simple fact that they didn't know, and jokes about the American Adventure being an air-conditioned nap.

During my undergraduate career, I took a class on public history in which much of the class, as the name suggests, was devoted to how historians can convey American history to the public in a way that is accessible to the most people but also accurate to the true events. In one such article for this class, the author cited Disney's American Adventure as a disgrace to the idea of public history. I understand where the author was coming from—if the show was to be put on an equal playing field as a day-long (or more) visit to a history museum, I would admit to seeing some issues with the show, but given its time restraint and placement in a theme park, I did not quite understand the author's utter disgust toward it. Plenty of portions of American history are overlooked by the show, but for a show that is less than 30 minutes long, I'm not sure how much we would reasonably expect to squeeze in while still including some level of information and storyline.

When I moved to Orlando to participate in the Disney College Program, and I saw the show on a much more regular basis, I not only began to research the speeches by those two figures, but of the entire show. I learned that the actual speech Frederick Douglass gave was very close to what is said during the show, and if anything, it was shortened to fit the timeframe. Chief Joseph's speech was more to the point in real life, and realistic in that he went into more detail on the condition of his people's suffering than his audio animatronic does in the show.

And yet, I wanted to learn more.

Now, when I walk through an ornately detailed queue in Frontierland, or consider the architecture in Hollywood Studios, I want to know how much of it is true. Even with only small hints of authentic details, I am inspired to dig deeper and understand what was in the minds of Imagineers when they were designing various locations, and regardless of their authenticity I'm ultimately inspired to learn more about different parts of history.

The debate about whether or not entertainment venues like theme parks should have any kind of authority in relaying history will likely continue for as long as the parks themselves exist, but the public interest in learning more beyond what we see in the parks should then continue as well.

Acknowledgments

Researching and writing this book would not have been possible without the support of my friends and family, including my parents; my grandparents; my fiancé, Charles Saldi; my friends Amy Regan, Theresa Colella, Cristian Perez, Nora Marimon, Natalie Bermudez, Anthony Figueroa, Natalie Martinez, and Aly Schmidt; and caffeination by DAVIDsTEA.

I would also like to extend my appreciation for the rest of the Disney fan community, including Disney historians who inspire me to continue researching and writing about these subjects: Jim Korkis, Didier Ghez, Jeff Kurtti, and David Smith, to name a few, along with Disney Imagineers like Marty Sklar and Joe Rohde whose design plans and attention to detail form the foundation of the areas of the parks I'm most interested in learning more about.

Lastly, I'd like to acknowledge the Disney College Program community, who provide me with so much support for my work on this book as well as on my blog, and of course with my contributing writers for castlepartyblog.com, Meghan Lemmo, Ashleigh Schneider, Caitlin Reddington, and Nicole Karnath.

About the Author

Brittany DiCologero has been researching the history of the Walt Disney World Resort since she learned how to read and write. Following her completion of coursework toward a bachelor of arts degree in History from St. Anselm College, she worked for the Walt Disney Company through the Disney College Program. She is also the author of *Brittany Earns Her Ears*, a memoir focusing on her experiences working in Animal Kingdom's DinoLand, U.S.A.

Currently, Brittany is a freelance writer for various travel and lifestyle websites, many of which focus on Disney including her own blog, castlepartyblog.com.

ABOUT THEME PARK PRESS

Theme Park Press publishes books primarily about the Disney company, its history, culture, films, animation, and theme parks, as well as theme parks in general.

Our authors include noted historians, animators, Imagineers, and experts in the theme park industry.

We also publish many books by first-time authors, with topics ranging from fiction to theme park guides.

And we're always looking for new talent. If you'd like to write for us, or if you're interested in the many other titles in our catalog, please visit:

www.ThemeParkPress.com

Theme Park Press Newsletter

Subscribe to our free email newsletter and enjoy:

- Free book downloads and giveaways
- Access to excerpts from our many books
- Announcements of forthcoming releases
- Exclusive additional content and chapters
- And more good stuff available nowhere else

To subscribe, visit www.ThemeParkPress.com, or send email to newsletter@themeparkpress.com.

Read more about these books
and our many other titles at:

www.ThemeParkPress.com

Made in the USA
Middletown, DE
25 August 2019